Active PE

Book 2

    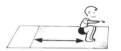

David Alldridge and Robert Fisher

SIMON & SCHUSTER
EDUCATION

© Robert Fisher and David Alldridge 1994

First published in the United Kingdom in 1994 by
Simon & Schuster Education
Campus 400, Maylands Avenue
Hemel Hempstead, Herts HP2 7EZ

Printed in the United Kingdom by Redwood Books, Trowbridge

A catalogue record of this book is available from the British Library

ISBN 0 7501 0552 6

Designed by Robert and Jean Wheeler Design Associates
Edited by Catherine Hardingham

Contents

Introduction

Active PE aims to help teachers of primary-age children to implement the National Curriculum in planning, teaching and assessing physical education (PE). Book 1 covers Key Stage 1: the 5–7 age range (years reception, 1 and 2), and Book 2 covers Key Stage 2: the 7–11+ age range (years 3–6). Active PE offers developing units of work which will be of practical use to teachers in helping children to enjoy and succeed in all aspects of PE.

About this book

The units of Book 2 offer a comprehensive and complete scheme of work for the six areas of study in PE for Key Stage 2: gymnastics, dance, games, athletics, outdoor education and swimming. The section on assessment includes record sheets to help evaluate progress, which can be photocopied and used as an ongoing record of achievement for each child. You will also find a list of resources at the end of the book, giving useful information about relevant publications, and useful addresses.

Gymnastics, dance and games are seen as the core areas of PE in the primary school and should be experienced regularly by children (weekly if possible) throughout the year. Athletics can often be linked to games, as many athletic skills fit easily into the games programme, especially running, jumping and throwing. Outdoor and adventurous activities ought, where possible, to be part of the daily experience of each child as outdoor play, and can be linked to many areas of learning. Swimming is an activity that schools may or may not choose to include at Key Stage 1, but it is a National Curriculum requirement that all children should have been taught to swim at least 25 metres by the end of Key Stage 2.

Active PE provides a broad-based PE programme that will help young children develop all aspects of the 'physical' child, and also help support social, conceptual and emotional development. The book shows how to present active, enjoyable and successful PE lessons, which will help children form positive attitudes to physical activity, and encourage lifelong health and fitness.

How to use this book

Each of the six units in this book contains the following sections: **What to teach** includes Statements of Attainment and Programmes of Study as outlined in the National Curriculum. These set out the statutory requirements in England and Wales for each teaching aspect of PE. This section provides a framework and reference point for long-term planning in PE, and for assessing the progress of individual children. Units of work are identified that aim to cover the Statements of Attainment and Programmes of Study for a year, or across a key stage. **Lesson planning** includes advice on how to prepare, organise and plan a lesson or series of lessons for each unit of work, within a suggested pattern of warm-up activity, skills development and conclusion. **Units of work** include themes and suggested activities which will help to develop knowledge, skills and positive attitudes in PE. The activities are listed under key themes, with activities which progress in a suggested order, from simple to more complex tasks. You are invited to select those tasks you consider most suitable for the children in your class. **Assessment** and record-keeping advice is given in the section pp167–183. **Resources** for each element of the PE curriculum are suggested in the section pp183–190. An **index** at the back of the book provides quick and easy reference to the key elements of PE-teaching contained in this book.

The **ACTIVE** in *Active PE* expresses the aims that we have in our teaching of PE, to offer children learning experiences that are:

A ctive	–	promoting healthy, active lifestyles.
C o-operative	–	teaching co-operation with others.
T houghtful	–	encouraging planning, reflection and review.
I nventive	–	fostering creativity in thought and movement.
V aried	–	developing a variety of physical skills.
E njoyable	–	gaining enjoyment from physical activity.

Why is PE important ?

There are many reasons why PE is important. These reasons can be summarised under three headings – the value of healthy exercise; the growth of physical intelligence; and the development of self-confidence.

The value of healthy exercise

One of the most important reasons for PE is that it provides children with exercise which will help develop:

- **Growth**: exercise is essential for physical growth, development and the healthy functioning of the various systems in the body.
- **Strength**: regular exercise leads to greater physical and muscular strength.

- **Suppleness**: varied experience of physical movements will increase suppleness, and the responsiveness of the body to physical challenge.
- **Stamina**: exercise improves the heart and cardiovascular system, which will help develop stamina and functional capacity.

Recent studies have revealed that many British children do not experience vigorous exercise in school, or in their out-of-school activities. This probably contributes to the low levels of fitness characteristic of many older schoolchildren. A priority for physical education is not only to ensure that children exercise, but to help build up an awareness of health issues and the value of an active lifestyle. The body is like a machine that stays healthy with use; it needs to be cared for, and the exercise habit is one that we hope will stay with them throughout life.

The growth of physical intelligence

Physical intelligence is made up of physical and mental skills (physical skills are more accurately called psycho-motor skills). These physical and mental skills are closely linked. Success in physical activity depends on intellectual skills such as concentration, judgement and close observation, as well as on creativity in thought and movement. Active PE means being active in mind and body; we need to encourage a thoughtful or 'mindful' approach to physical activity, including an awareness of self and of others. This has important practical consequences, since safety of self and others is best achieved through a 'think first' approach.

(For more on physical and other forms of intelligence see *Teaching Children to Think* by Robert Fisher, published by Simon & Schuster)

The development of self-confidence

The body is not simply a machine. It is a vehicle of a child's sense of self and self-worth. The uniqueness of the children's bodies is a reflection of their uniqueness as individuals. In making PE lessons enjoyable and satisfying, in providing opportunities for success and development of skills, we also help to build self-esteem and a sense of self-worth. Through PE we can give children physical confidence. We help to show them that they can do more than they think, and that they can do things well. In our lessons we value who they are and what they can achieve. Studies have shown the value of building self-esteem and high expectations in the development of positive attitudes to life and learning. A growing sense of confidence and physical control can help children to respond well to other forms of challenge, both in and out of school.

Fig 1: Some aims of physical education

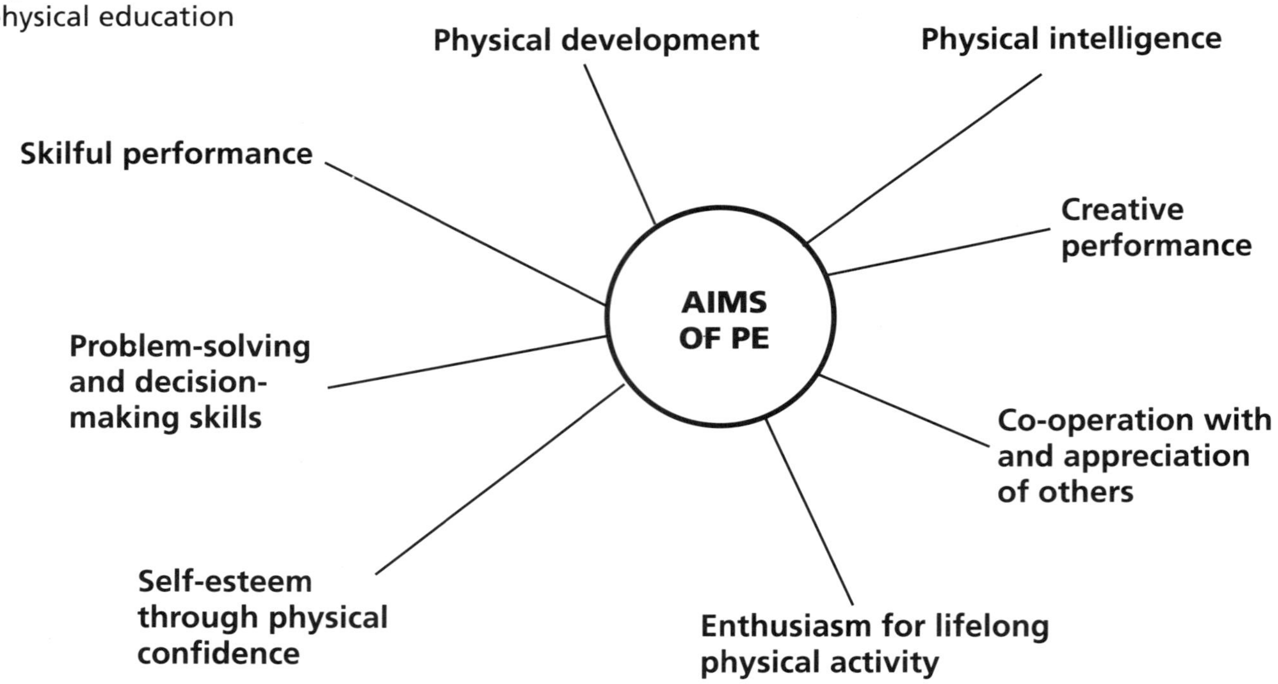

Physical development

Physical intelligence

Skilful performance

Creative performance

AIMS OF PE

Problem-solving and decision-making skills

Co-operation with and appreciation of others

Self-esteem through physical confidence

Enthusiasm for lifelong physical activity

What should we teach ?

PE and the National Curriculum

The National Curriculum defines the basic entitlement of pupils to PE under three component headings:

- One attainment target (AT).
- End of key stage statements (EKSS).
- Programmes of study (PoS).

The attainment target

Physical Education in the National Curriculum (1992) states that the one attainment target for PE for pupils aged 5–16 shall be that 'pupils should be able to demonstrate the knowledge, skills and understanding involved in areas of activity encompassing athletic activities, dance, games, gymnastic activities, outdoor and adventurous activities and swimming'. This attainment target relates to the three basic processes of planning, performing and evaluating (plan-do-review) which should relate to all purposeful physical activity: **planning** involves thinking ahead, exploring options, setting goals, selecting, organising, creating and structuring physical practice; **performing** involves active participation, copying, practising, repeating, implementing a plan of action, refining, adapting, developing, improving and improvising; **evaluating** involves observing, describing (using word and action), analysing, comparing and contrasting, judging, reviewing, and recognising the effects of physical activities on their bodies.

These processes are expressed in the end of key stage statements which relate to the programme of study for Key Stage 2. Pupils should be able to:

- plan, practise, improve and remember more complex sequences of movement;
- perform effectively in activities requiring quick decision-making;
- respond safely, alone and with others, to challenging tasks, taking account of levels of skill and understanding;
- swim unaided for at least 25 metres and demonstrate an understanding of water safety;
- evaluate how well they and others perform and behave against criteria suggested by the teacher, and suggest ways of improving performance;
- sustain energetic activity over appropriate periods of time in a range of physical activities and understand the effects of exercise on the body.

(PE in the National Curriculum, 1992)

Programme of Study (PoS)

These define both general requirements about what the pupils should have opportunities to learn and experience, as well as the specific areas of activity:

- gymnastics;
- games;
- athletics;
- dance;
- outdoor and adventurous activity;
- swimming.

The general statements in the PoS reflect the importance within PE of three elements which should permeate all activities:

Personal and social development

In order to help pupils become independent learners, they should be encouraged to solve for themselves the problems they encounter in the course of physical activities. In order to develop positive attitudes, pupils should be encouraged to observe the conventions of fair play, honest competition and good sporting behaviour; understand and cope with a variety of outcomes, including success and failure; and be aware of the effects and consequences of their actions on others and on the environment.

Safety

To help ensure safe practice, pupils should be taught to:

- be concerned with their own and others' safety in all activities;

- understand the safety risks of wearing inappropriate clothing, footwear and jewellery;
- lift, carry and place equipment safely;
- respond readily to instructions and signals within established routines and follow relevant rules and codes.

Health-related exercise

In PE lessons pupils should be taught to:

- be physically active;
- engage in activities that involve the whole body, maintain flexibility and develop strength and endurance;
- adopt good posture and the correct use of the body at all times.

Planning for PE

Active PE is designed to support planning for PE at all levels, including a scheme of work to cover the whole key stage; shorter units of work, for example, a PE programme for a school term or year; or lesson plans for a particular class or group. A scheme of work can be divided into units of work, which can be taught in a variety of ways, for example, through weekly timetabled lessons; a block of time, eg swimming each day for three to four weeks; or as part of a cross-curricular theme, eg dance and drama, or environmental study outdoor visits.

Each area of activity does not need an equal share of curriculum time, provided that all areas of the PoS have been covered by the end of the key stage. At Key Stages 1 and 2 it is recommended that emphasis be placed on gymnastics, dance and games in order to create a basic repertoire of movement skills and understanding. Athletics and outdoor activities will need less time at these key stages. The organisation of swimming in individual schools will be influenced by the availability of pool facilities, transport and teacher expertise. There is evidence to suggest that swimming is best learnt through short but intensive participation, eg swimming every day for a month.

Important aspects of planning will include breadth and balance, progression, differentiation to meet individual needs, assessment and record-keeping.

Breadth and balance

Breadth and balance can be provided by a combination of:

- games/athletics, gymnastics, dance, and outdoor/adventurous activities;
- competitive and non-competitive activity;
- contact and non-contact activity;

• group, pair and individual activity;
• emphasis on developing physical skill and on tactical understanding;
• use of different teaching approaches (see below).

Fig 2: An example of a PE programme at Key Stage 2

Teachers will need to respond to local circumstances, school traditions and children's needs in planning their programme. The following is one possible framework for PE at Key Stage 2:

	Year 3			Year 4			Year 5			Year 6		
	Aut	Sp	Sum	Aut	Sp	Sum	Aut	Sp	Sum	Aut	Sp	Sum
Gymnastics	✔	✔	✔	✔✔	✔	✔	✔	✔	✔	✔	✔	✔✔ *(includes fitness activities)*
Dance		✔✔	✔	✔	✔	✔	✔	✔	✔	✔✔	✔✔	
Games	✔✔	✔✔	✔✔	✔✔	✔✔	✔✔	✔✔	✔✔	✔✔	✔✔	✔✔	✔✔
Swimming	✔		✔	✔✔	✔		✔		✔✔	✔	✔	✔
Athletics	✔		✔	✔		✔✔	✔	✔	✔✔	✔		✔✔
Outdoor/ Adventurous			✔		✔				✔	✔	✔	✔

On-going as part of cross-curricular work in Geography, Science, Environmental Education ←——→

✔ = represents half a term

N.B.

1. Aim for 3 or 4 lessons per week, if possible, to ensure breadth and balance.

2. Other activities across the curriculum can ensure some physical activity daily, eg drama, RE/drama, use of play area/frame, active playtimes, outdoor education, maths/science trails.

Notes:

1. 3 or 4 sessions of PE allocated weekly.

2. Half hour weekly for **Gymnastics and Dance,** half to one hour for Games, Swimming, Athletics.

3. Dance could well link with **dance/drama** activity.

4. Swimming. For practical purposes (transport and ability range) Y3 + Y5, Y4 + Y6 have been linked together.

5. Use has been made of September and October, March and April for **Athletics** activities.

6. Additional time in **Outdoor/Adventurous** activities has been allocated in Years 4–6 for day, week-end (residential), week (residential) adventurous activities.

No two schools will organise their PE programme identically, there are too many variables. The example above may help your planning and ensure **breadth and balance** in your PE programme.

With whole-school planning, imagination and flexibility we can ensure children receive a balanced programme in PE.

Progression

Children develop at different rates, so rate of progress in PE will vary and may be affected by illness, accident or absence. Children who are injured or otherwise excused from PE can still participate in some aspect of the work, for example, reporting on or evaluating the progress of others, by recording activity eg through drawing, or devising rules for a game. Children's development in PE will involve progression from:

- Dependence to independence, eg 'Can you find another way to balance?'
- Repeating given tasks, to creating and structuring their own, eg 'Roll to finish in different positions of balance.'
- Using given criteria to judge performance, to developing their own criteria for identifying a 'good' performance, eg 'Can you say or show why you think it is a good movement ?'
- Simple activities, to more complex activities and sequences, eg' Join two rolls with a hands to feet movement.'
- Natural movement, to skilful/aesthetic performance, eg 'Now can you roll in a tucked position and finish in a high stretch shape?'

The elements of progress are difficulty, and quality in the planning, performing and evaluation of physical activities. Progress in levels of difficulty can be achieved by asking for:

- Greater variety in movements within a task, eg 'Can you jump higher/extend your body further?'
- Improved performance in movement, eg 'Can you show me a better shape?'
- Improved co-ordination of movements, eg 'Can you change from one shape to another/link one movement to another?'

Differentiation

Planning for PE means seeking to cater for a range of different abilities and needs. This will mean making provision for groups of children with similar needs, and for those with individual or special needs. This is a demanding task, best achieved by:

- building on the past achievements of individual pupils;
- planning to develop specific skills, knowledge and understanding;
- encouraging participation of those with physical impairment or special needs;
- providing opportunities for each child to be challenged and to experience success.

Strategies should include:

differentiation by task: children working through a series of activities with increasing levels of difficulty, eg catching with two hands/one hand/left hand/right hand;

differentiation by outcome: children engaged on a common task which allows for different levels of response, eg creating a dance to the same piece of music.

Children with special needs

Children with special needs have an entitlement to a broad and balanced PE programme relevant to those needs. The best results are achieved by matching tasks and resources to the needs of the pupils. If the task is too difficult the pupil will fail. If it is too easy the pupil will succeed with little satisfaction or skill development. Strategies that help in meeting special needs include:

- breaking down an activity into small achievable steps;
- adapting and simplifying tasks so that success can be achieved;
- presenting an activity slowly and clearly;
- demonstrating or modelling an activity;
- encouraging work with a sympathetic partner.

An effective programme will involve planning for differentiation by providing:
- a variety of resources for different levels of ability;
- a variety of grouping – individual, pairs, groups (sometimes according to ability);
- a variety of tasks, using different allocations of time, different roles and expectations.

For more on children with special needs in PE see p181.

Assessment

Teachers should use the end of key stage statements as reference points for assessment in PE. There are not the levels of attainment that are common to most other foundation subjects, and it is important, therefore, for teachers to keep their own continuing assessments of pupils' progress in PE. The gathering of evidence will include observation, recording and reporting.

Observation is the most obvious way of collecting evidence in PE. Children should be encouraged to use self-assessment, and opportunities provided for them, to observe, evaluate and communicate on their own and each other's performance. Observers might be asked to look for variety, eg 'How many different ways?' or for quality, eg 'Can you pick out something good in what you see?'.

Recording of evidence over a period of time is important, so that evidence of achievement and progress is noted throughout the key stage, and not just left to the end.

Reporting should reflect the positive achievements of each child in each area of the PoS. Schools can select their own format for reporting to parents, for example, either a general comment on attainment and progress, or specific comments and levels of attainment. At the end of the key stage there is, of course, a statutory requirement to report with reference to the EKSS. Records should be kept to a minimum, so as not to be time-consuming or interfere with teaching. For more on assessment and examples of record sheets see pp167–182.

Managing the PE lesson

In organising and managing a PE lesson*, key factors such as communication, discipline, safety and equal opportunities will need consideration.

Communication

Important elements of good communication include:

- **Being prepared**: plan what is to be said, prepare the resources, be clear about the aims of the lesson, be aware of the needs of the children. Make a plan of the lesson on paper, or note key points on a card, or in your head if you have a good memory!
- **Being clear**: stand where all can see you, emphasise key points, repeat if necessary (or check understanding by asking them to tell you). Avoid asking vague questions like 'Shall we...? Would you like to...?'; make statements instead like 'We are going to...'
- **Being simple**: use simple language; rephrase if necessary, do not talk too much (children want to move!). Use a simple signal for 'stop' and 'go', use gestures to reinforce your message.
- **Being vivid**: vary the voice, be enthusiastic. Speak quietly sometimes (when you have full attention), project your voice sometimes, eg to praise a child across the room; put feeling into your voice.
- **Being natural**: successful PE teaching can be defined as 'grace under pressure'; being natural and relaxed is not easy when you are organising large numbers of children. Tell the children how you feel (it will help them to understand you), and try the relaxing effect of a smile or laugh.

Discipline

The management of the PE lesson begins in the classroom or in the changing room. Remind children about the rules and routines before they begin to change. Walk with care and poise to the PE area and check that they are in their agreed positions, or know their first activity, before you begin. Practise the routines that make for a smooth PE lesson: keep all the chidren in view all the time; remind the children of the three or four basic rules that you have agreed and deal firmly with 'rule-breakers'.

*For more on class management see *Teaching Juniors* by Robert Fisher (Simon & Schuster) pp28–55.

Constantly encourage positive behaviour and expect high standards. Be clear about the noise level you will permit; make them work silently if you think this will aid their concentration and effort. Anticipate problems by keeping them actively involved in what they are doing and don't punish groups or the whole class for the misdemeanours of individuals. Try to catch them being good: praise good behaviour and effort. Remember, the lesson does not end until they have changed and are back in the classroom.

Safety

The safety of the children should be the first concern in any activity: be aware of the safety code of the school; know what to do in an emergency and identify the member(s) of staff responsible for first-aid. Check that equipment is stable and in good condition and that ground surfaces are clean and free from obstacles. Walls should be free from protrusions, especially sharp edges, and ensure that there is sufficient space for the children to work in. If an accident occurs, stop whatever is going on and ask the children to sit quietly. If necessary, ask a child to fetch another adult. The first rule of first-aid is: if in doubt, don't. Always follow the accident procedures of the school.

Equal opportunities

Every child has an entitlement to PE. This means that children should not be denied PE as a punishment, although they may be withdrawn from an activity during the lesson if their behaviour is dangerous, or they are denying opportunities for others. All children should be allowed access to the activities of the lesson, eg in putting out apparatus.

Avoid situations which create gender differentiation or stereotyping, such as boys' groups and girls' groups. Try not to use sexist or gender-related language, such as 'Boys march like soldiers. Girls dance like ballet dancers'. Boys and girls should have access to all games, and to all kinds of equipment.

Just as we avoid gender bias, we should also beware of cultural or racial bias. Much can be learnt from the sports and physical activities practised in differing ethnic and cultural groups. PE has an important role to play in every society; our physical activity helps us to define who we are. So what teaching strategies should we use?

Teaching approaches and learning opportunities

Children have different needs and abilities, but all need the opportunity to plan, perform and review their physical activities. There is no one right way to teach PE. To achieve success we need to use different teaching approaches to match the needs of different activities, individual children and changing circumstances. The following teaching strategies can be adapted to help children explore, invent, plan, perform, enjoy, observe and review their actions – to experience **active PE**.

- **Experimenting**: through providing apparatus or equipment for children to play freely, discover their abilities and how to use their expressive physical qualities. For very young children, such play is essential for early development. Older children also need these opportunities when introduced to new activities, or when confidence is lacking. Children with special needs may benefit from more extended opportunities for experimental play.
- **Problem-solving**: through giving children problems to investigate, for example: How many different ways can you move along (or across) a bench? Explore different ways to roll a ball. How can you move through these hoops without touching them? Can you roll on the mat without touching anyone else in the group with two, three or four rolling at one time?
- **Task-setting**: through a specific task being set by the teacher or by the children, for example: balance on two hands and one foot; jump with a big stretch before landing; take your weight on your hands and kick up one/two feet.
- **Skill-teaching**: through a skill being taught by means of exposition or demonstration, or a combination of both ('show and tell'). Breaking the skill down into short steps can be helpful; also rehearsing what you are about to do, talking through what you are showing, and inviting or asking questions. This also reflects the old teaching strategy of 'tell 'em before they do it, tell 'em while they are doing it, and tell 'em after they have done it.'

After a short period of experimentation, most children will benefit from a degree of skill training. Children should also be encouraged to invent new ideas or movements for others to try, to share skills with each other and learn to appreciate each other's efforts. A balance between these approaches will help to ensure that all children are active and achieve success at their own level.

PE links across the curriculum

PE has important contributions to make across the curriculum: to cross-curricular skills such as communication and problem-solving; to cross-curricular themes such as health education, environmental and social education; and to common themes in all areas of the curriculum. The following chart shows some of the cross-curricular perspectives of PE:

Fig 3: PE: a cross-curricular perspective

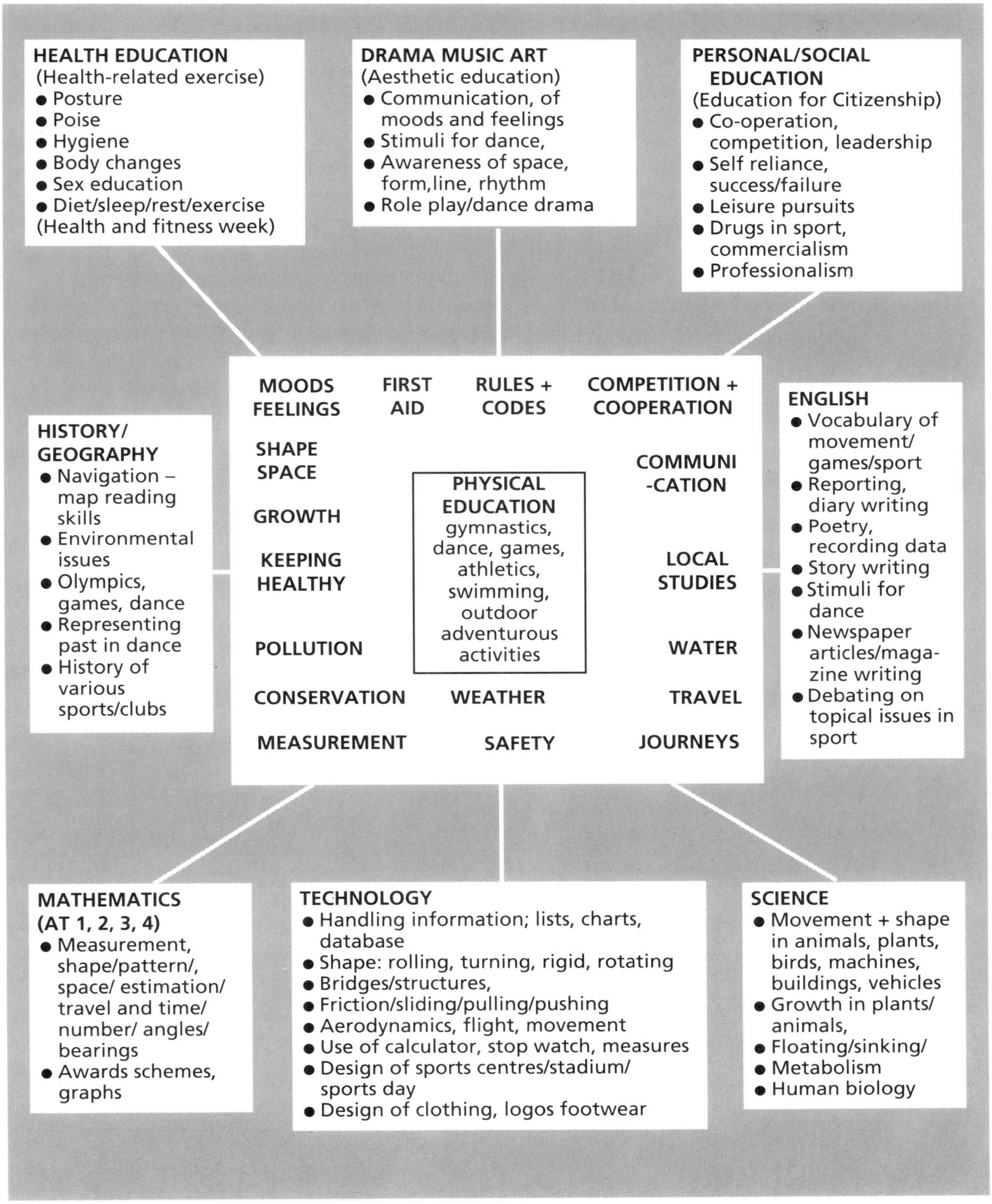

HEALTH EDUCATION
(Health-related exercise)
- Posture
- Poise
- Hygiene
- Body changes
- Sex education
- Diet/sleep/rest/exercise
(Health and fitness week)

DRAMA MUSIC ART
(Aesthetic education)
- Communication, of moods and feelings
- Stimuli for dance,
- Awareness of space, form, line, rhythm
- Role play/dance drama

PERSONAL/SOCIAL EDUCATION
(Education for Citizenship)
- Co-operation, competition, leadership
- Self reliance, success/failure
- Leisure pursuits
- Drugs in sport, commercialism
- Professionalism

HISTORY/ GEOGRAPHY
- Navigation – map reading skills
- Environmental issues
- Olympics, games, dance
- Representing past in dance
- History of various sports/clubs

MOODS FEELINGS   FIRST AID   RULES + CODES   COMPETITION + COOPERATION

SHAPE SPACE

GROWTH

KEEPING HEALTHY

PHYSICAL EDUCATION
gymnastics, dance, games, athletics, swimming, outdoor adventurous activities

COMMUNI -CATION

LOCAL STUDIES

POLLUTION

CONSERVATION   WEATHER

WATER

TRAVEL

MEASUREMENT   SAFETY   JOURNEYS

ENGLISH
- Vocabulary of movement/ games/sport
- Reporting, diary writing
- Poetry, recording data
- Story writing
- Stimuli for dance
- Newspaper articles/maga-zine writing
- Debating on topical issues in sport

MATHEMATICS
(AT 1, 2, 3, 4)
- Measurement, shape/pattern/, space/ estimation/ travel and time/ number/ angles/ bearings
- Awards schemes, graphs

TECHNOLOGY
- Handling information; lists, charts, database
- Shape: rolling, turning, rigid, rotating
- Bridges/structures,
- Friction/sliding/pulling/pushing
- Aerodynamics, flight, movement
- Use of calculator, stop watch, measures
- Design of sports centres/stadium/ sports day
- Design of clothing, logos footwear

SCIENCE
- Movement + shape in animals, plants, birds, machines, buildings, vehicles
- Growth in plants/ animals,
- Floating/sinking/
- Metabolism
- Human biology

Active in body and mind

What we are developing and assessing in PE is an important aspect of a child's development – that of physical intelligence. It is part of the problem-solving, and expressive or creative capacity of human life. Carrying out a dance sequence or hitting a tennis ball are not problems in a logical or linguistic sense; they are problems demanding physical intelligence, involving use of both mind and body. Even the simplest of human actions can involve skill and grace and can present real physical challenge. The exhiliration of success, the widening range of physical skill and a growing awareness of one's own body and self – all these and more can be provided by PE.

In writing about the need to combine body and mind in tennis, Tim Gallwey (1976) observed: 'To return an average serve, you have about a second to do this. To hit the ball at all is remarkable and yet not uncommon. The truth is that everyone who inhabits a human body possesses a remarkable creation'. It is to help our children make the most of their 'remarkable creation' that we seek to make the most out of their physical education lessons, to fulfil the potential of an active body and mind. As one child observed after a PE lesson: 'I didn't know I can do it until I done it. I wonder if I can do something I can't do next time?'

Gymnastics

'Gymnastics is when you have to think about the way you move'.
'Gymnastics are ways of moving your body so it looks good and feels good'.
'Gymnastics is when you tell your body to do things in PE that it hasn't done before'.

(Junior children describing gymnastics)

By the age of seven children should have had much experience of basic gymnastic activity. From seven to eleven years they should repeat and develop further ways of travelling, turning, rolling, jumping, balancing, swinging and taking weight on different parts of the body.

Gymnastics lessons in school should provide experience of many ways of performing these basic actions and should give children opportunities to practise, adapt, and improve control of their individual actions. As they become more physically skilled and confident, they should be given opportunities to link together a series of actions, both on the floor and on apparatus, and be encouraged to repeat them at different levels and speeds. They should increasingly work with partners, for example in activities that involve following, copying, mirroring, creating shapes and sequences, as obstacles and as observers. They should also be taught as part of the programme to carry and position gymnastic apparatus using the correct lifting technique in co-operation with others. This section on gymnastics provides a guide to the following:

• What to teach.
• Lesson planning.
• Themes for developing skills in gymnastics.
• Games activities.

What to teach

gymnastics in the National Curriculum

Gymnastic activities focus on the body. They are concerned with acquiring control, co-ordination and versatility in the use of the body, and responding to challenges.

The Statements of Attainment in the National Curriculum say that at the end of Key Stage 2, when pupils are eleven years old, they should be able to:
- plan, practise, improve and remember more complex sequences of movement;
- perform effectively in activities requiring quick decision making;
- respond safely, alone and with others, to challenging tasks, taking account of levels of skill and understanding;
- evaluate how well they and others perform and behave against criteria suggested by the teacher and suggest ways of improving performance;
- sustain energetic activity over appropriate periods of time in a range of physical activities and understand the effects of exercise on the body;
- swim unaided for at least 25 metres and demonstrate an understanding of water safety.

The Programmes of Study for gymnastics say that pupils should:

- be enabled, on floor or apparatus, to find more ways to: jump, roll, swing, balance, take weight on hands, and adapt, practice and refine these actions;
- be guided to perform in a controlled manner and to understand that the ending of one action can become the beginning of the next;
- be given opportunities on floor and apparatus in response to set tasks, to explore, select, develop, practise and refine a longer series of actions, making increasingly complex movement sequences which they are able to repeat;
- be enabled to respond to a variety of tasks, alone or with a partner, emphasising changing shape, speed and direction through gymnastic actions;
- continue to be taught to carry and position apparatus and adopt correct lifting techniques.

Lesson planning

'What I like to do is to rehearse in my mind exactly what I'm going to do in a PE lesson. Changing first helps to get me in the right frame of mind – and shows the children I mean business!' *(student teacher)*

The key to success in teaching gymnastics is careful planning which should cover the half-term or term ahead to allow continuity and progression in gymnastic experience. The following themes provide guidance on what to include in a programme of lessons. Links should also be made with classroom topics where appropriate.

Preparing for the PE lesson

The PE lesson begins in the classroom; not the gymnastics of course, but preparation for what in the past was called 'gym'. Time can be taken to review key points from the last lesson. Reminders can be given about how to walk to the hall or PE location. In planning the lesson look for links with classwork (see cross-curricular links p17). Think about the apparatus required: is it spaced conveniently around the edge of the hall for later moving and use?

Fig 4: Apparatus spaced around the hall perimeter.

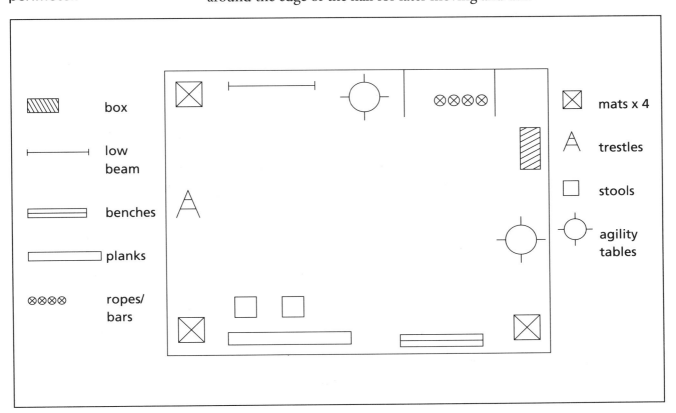

One way to prepare is to be changed yourself – at least by wearing PE shoes. The lesson begins when changing starts, and ends when changing finishes. What children change out of and into is a matter of school policy, but it does not have to be an individual activity; they can change in pairs to help each other; try timing them to speed them up.

Organising the apparatus

When apparatus is used you will need to consider the children's age and ability to handle the equipment.

You will need to link your use of the apparatus with previous groups, or the next group in the hall. It is important for children to begin to handle and move the apparatus (planks, stools, mats, forms, etc) at an early age, providing it is safe and they adopt the correct lifting techniques and are physically able to do so. Choose light, adaptable equipment (see Resources p184). Part of PE is learning about the apparatus or equipment, what each piece is called, how it is used and how it may be moved and fixed for safety.

Apparatus should be moved by children as part of the lesson, starting with benches, mats, planks, box-tops and tables. All groups should have responsibility for moving apparatus; spending time on handling the apparatus in the early stages will pay dividends later. Try to maintain a firm, well-organised and methodical approach. The following are some points to consider:

- use two or four children as the handling group for each piece of apparatus;
- teach a good lifting position, with straight backs and bent knees;
- teach children to lift apparatus into position; don't drag apparatus or mats across the floor;
- praise and show good practice every lesson (use a good group to demonstrate);
- move apparatus one or two pieces at a time (handled by one or two groups);
- move more apparatus at a time as competence grows (eg half the class at a time, progressing to the whole class);
- move apparatus from/to sides of the hall to designated positions for ease and speed of access;
- discuss in the classroom the safe carrying of apparatus, and other heavy loads;
- discuss the position of apparatus in class (eg by using a chart on the wall).

It can be useful, and revealing, to note the time taken for putting out (and putting away) the apparatus. Safety rather than speed is the keynote, but having an achievable target time of about two to three minutes to complete the operation may be useful.

Using the apparatus

In planning for work on the large apparatus, your aim should be to reduce as far as possible the time children spend queueing for their turn (this wastes their time and can encourage poor behaviour). But with a large number of children how do you keep everyone active? Points to consider include the **positioning of mats** to encourage maximum participation, **varying the approach to and landing from** apparatus, and the **use of adjacent floor space.** The diagrams below show the importance of positioning of mats and apparatus to allow for a variety of approaches to and landings from apparatus.

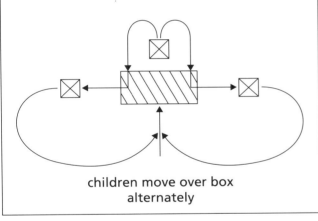

Fig 5: A group of five children active on a box, with three mats (jumping, vaulting, landing)

children move over box alternately

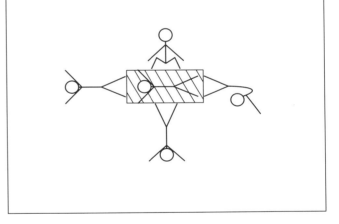

Fig 6: Five children showing positions of balance on and around a box or table

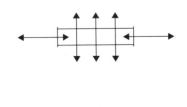

Fig 7: Five children active on a balance bench (transfer of weight, hands and feet)

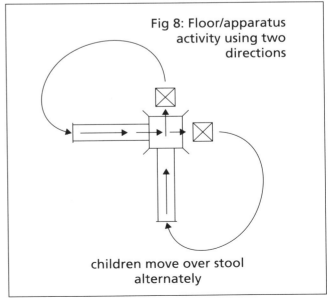

Fig 8: Floor/apparatus activity using two directions

children move over stool alternately

The following diagrams show examples of layouts of apparatus designed for maximum activity and use of available space.

Fig 9: Using benches and box tops or tables

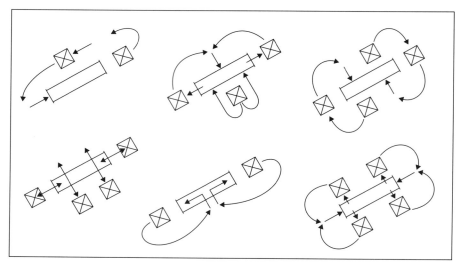

- Use for themes of: travel and space, weight transfer, pathways.
- Four or five per team, all active.
- Encourage groups to invent new patterns of movement over benches.

Fig 10: Using varied apparatus

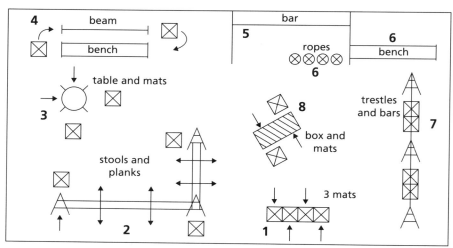

- Use for all themes.
- Groups can rotate in sequence, group by group.
  or
- Choose freely with ropes/bars group controlled (max four or five per activity).

Planning a lesson

In most schools, gymnastic sessions for junior children last 25–30 minutes. A basic plan for a lesson might be:

1. **Introduction/warm up** (2–3 minutes) to prepare the body for later activity. It should be vigorous, challenging and fun, setting the tone of the lesson in controlled purposeful activity, as soon as the children enter the hall (eg lots of running, jumping, pair games, class games and stretching activities).
2. **Floorwork** (8–10 minutes): a theme explored and developed through tasks set by teacher.
3. **Apparatus** (10–12 minutes): a theme developed using small equipment or large apparatus.
4. **Conclusion** (4–5 minutes): apparatus cleared, and a quiet, controlled activity related to earlier floorwork, or a class game involving control and concentration.

It is not necessary for there to be floorwork and apparatus work for each lesson; an alternative model might be, for example, on different days:

Day 1: warm-up + floorwork + conclusion;

Day 2: warm up + develop on apparatus + conclusion.

Fig 11: During the lesson points to remember:

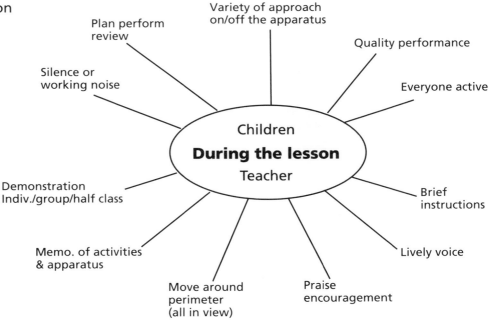

Each lesson should have a theme through which gymnastic skills can be explored and developed. The following are six themes, each of which could form the basis of a series of lessons or unit of work in PE.

Themes

The following themes provide a framework for ensuring that the Programmes of Study are implemented:

- **Travelling** involving use of space: jumping, rolling, springing, landing, climbing, sliding, and swinging.
- **Body shape:** curling, stretching, twisting, symmetrical, assymmetrical, together/apart.
- **Balance and supporting body weight:** balance, weight on hands, hanging.
- **Transferring body weight:** circling, turning, rocking, rolling, lifting, lowering, twisting.
- **Linking movements:** sequences of movement, balance and continuity.
- **Partner work and group work:** following, copying, matching, mirroring, supporting, planning and evaluating.

These themes should be developed and extended using different shapes (symmetrical and asymmetrical) and on different parts of the body, with special reference to **space** (personal and general); **levels/distance**; **speed**; **direction**; and **lightness/force**. By exploring and developing these aspects of each theme, interest and challenge can be maintained throughout Key Stage 2. The progressive tasks suggested within each theme can be developed each year to broaden experience, improve quality and provide challenge for children of all abilities.

The themes are explored with a list of developing activities which contain enough basic material for you to plan lessons covering up to half a term (six weeks). Each theme follows the warm up/floorwork/apparatus/conclusion pattern recommended earlier. Focus on one or two activities from each section in each lesson to which children will respond at their own level.

Travelling (or use of space)

Travelling involving use of space involves different ways of moving using the feet, or hands and feet, or large parts of the body (like tummy and bottom). Focus on developing awareness of:

- the space between individuals;
- the space needed to move safely (personal working space);
- the space in relation to directions, pathways and levels (general space around you);
- travelling: rolling, walking, running, climbing, skipping, jumping, springing, swinging and flying, dropping, sliding.

Introduction and warm up

The following are some introductory warm-up activities involving travel and use of space:

- Walk/jog/run using all the space in the hall. Stop on given signal.
- Walk/jog/run in different directions. Stop in a balanced shape: small/big/twisted, etc.
- Run in different directions: forwards, sideways, backwards (keep a free space around you).
- Jog or run at different speeds; stop in your own time, or on signal.
- Find different ways to travel on your feet; freeze on signal.
- Skip/jump/run in different directions. Stop in an 'action photograph'.
- Move in different directions on hands and feet.
- Move on other body parts, keeping space around you. Change body parts on signal.
- Walk/move in a confined space without touching each other.
- Jump high to occupy lots of space and make a controlled landing (a).

(a)

- Jump high to occupy as little space as possible.
- Run, jump and land. Be still.
- Find different ways to slide/push/pull/roll body across floor.
- Move under/around half the class who hold positions of balance (such as bridge shapes). Remember no touching other children!
- Use any of the Games activities (see p43).
- Use a variety of stretching exercises (see p77).
- Years 5 and 6 can use all or part of an exercise circuit (see pp77–78).

Floorwork

The following are some floorwork activities involving travel and use of space:

- Move freely about the hall on one, two, three or four body parts.
- First rock, then find different ways to roll your body.

(b)

- Roll across a mat in different ways and directions; practise changing your finishing position (b).
- Roll on the floor slowly, stand and travel on feet or other parts.
- Create a pattern of jumps; in a small space; in a large space.
- Jump, land and roll, then stop.
- Jump with a twist, land, and roll to sitting, kneeling, or standing finish.
- Find different ways to link a jump, a roll, and a hands and feet movement, then finish in a shape.
- Move from hands to feet across a small space or a large space.
- Find different ways to link together a hands to feet movement, a roll and a jump.

Small apparatus (hoops, ropes, beanbags)

The following are some activities using small apparatus to explore travel and use of space. Small apparatus may be used as a) objects to avoid; b) objects to move into; or c) objects to move away from.

(c)

- Move/jump/spring over or around a rope shape or a hoop.
- Travel across the floor, placing the hoop or rope to jump or move into or over.
- Balance as you walk along a rope placed on the floor.
- Crouch inside a hoop, spring to roll outside the hoop.
- Roll into a large hoop and stop.
- Find ways to move through a hoop held vertically by a partner (c).
- Ask children to invent more ways to travel using hoops, ropes and beanbags.

Travelling

The following are some activities using benches, low tables, box tops and mats (see figure 9, p24) to explore travel and space:

- Move on, along and off the apparatus quietly, without touching anyone else.
- Walk/hop/move quickly forwards, backwards, sideways; jump from the middle or end of the box to a controlled landing.
- Move along the bench forwards or backwards using hands and feet.

(d)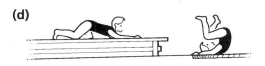

- slide, by pushing or pulling, along the surface of the apparatus; roll on to a mat from a prone position (d).
- Zigzag along a bench by bunny-jumping your legs from side to side over the bench.
- Move along the apparatus by twisting or turning; jump to land from the end or middle, then roll on mat.
- Jump across and over, or from, a bench to land and roll.
- Roll across or over a bench or box top (e).

(e)

- Move across benches in different ways, using hands and feet, and without touching the top.
- Move forwards, backwards or sideways across a box top or bench.
- Join together three movements along or across apparatus and over a mat.

Large apparatus

The following are some activities using a variety of large apparatus (see figure 10, p24) to explore travel and use of space:

(f)

- Move on and off the apparatus slowly, without touching others.
- Find different places to climb on, move along or over and then climb off the apparatus (f).
- Find different ways to move under, over and through the apparatus.
- Move over or along the apparatus using hands and feet.
- Spring on and off at the same place, slowly and with control.
- Find different ways to get on the apparatus: jump, spring, forwards, backwards, feet first, seat first, etc.
- Find different ways to get off the apparatus; hands first, backwards, forwards, sideways, with a roll.
- Find different ways to turn, roll, circle on the apparatus (g).

- Travel across the floor on to the apparatus, and jump to a controlled landing on the floor.
- Link three or four movements between two pieces of apparatus. Vary their shape and speed.
- With a partner. Make a sequence of a) matching, b) opposite movements with reference to space used, or speed and shape of movements.

(g)

Conclusion

After apparatus has been moved away:

- Practise a way to travel quietly/lightly across the floor.
- Find different ways to roll to a variety of finishing positions.
- Use one of the games activities on p43.
- Move silently in a small or large space. Freeze on signal.

Body shape

Body shape involves curling and stretching, twisting and turning. Children should be taught the contrast between these movements, symmetrical and assymetrical shapes, and to ways of changing direction while changing body shape.

Introduction and warm up

The following are some introductory/warm-up activities that explore body shape:

(h)

(i)

- Run freely about the space. Stop in curl/stretch/long/wide shape.
- Run and jump and show different shapes in the air.
- Move across the floor while curled/stretched.
- Run in a bent, tucked position with your fingers skimming the floor (h).
- Walk or run in a crouched position (i).
- Keep changing your body shape on the spot. Freeze on signal.
- Jump/hop on the spot to show different shapes in the air.
- In pairs. Follow and match a) partner's movements; b) partner's shape (not necessarily with same movements).
- Show symmetrical and assymetrical shapes while jumping on the spot from one or two feet.
- Use any of the warm-up games and activities on p43.
- Use a variety of the stretching activities on p77.
- Years 5 and 6 can use the exercise circuit on pp77–78.

Floorwork

The following are some floorwork activities that explore body shape:

- Weight on back/bottom/tummy, curl then stretch arms/legs wide.
- Weight on hands and feet to make curled/stretched/twisted shape.
- Make a stretched bridge shape using two, three, four or more body parts.
- Roll on to different body parts in curled, then stretched positions.
- Stretch, curl, roll on to another body part. Repeat.
- Weight on hands, kick up legs in curled, then stretched shapes.
- Curl up on back, stretch out into curled/stretched/twisted shapes on two, three, four or more body parts (j).

(j)

Stretch (5 parts touching floor)   curled   twist   Stretch (3 parts touching floor)

- Show different positions of symmetry and assymetry.
- Weight on hands, move feet to make stretched/ twisted/ symmetrical/assymetrical shapes.
- Repeat above with feet as central point, moving hands to vary body shape.
- Weight on one, two, three, four or more body parts to make twisted/symmetrical/assymetrical shapes.
- Move across the floor with body curled/stretched.

- Move across the floor changing from curled to stretched positions.
- Show different shapes while rolling: curled/symmetrical/assymetrical.
- Show different shapes while rolling; end in tucked/stretched/ symmetrical/assymetrical shape.
- Move on hands and feet symmetrically/assymetrically (k).
  - Move across the floor joining symmetrical and assymetrical movements.
  - Make a sequence showing positions of curl, stretch and twist; link with different rolls.

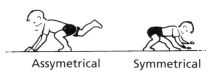

(k)   Assymetrical   Symmetrical

Small apparatus

The previous activities can also involve the use of small apparatus in exploring body shape. Hoops, ropes and beanbags can be used as objects to avoid; objects to reach; or objects to move into or over.

Large apparatus

You can use either a simple layout, such as figure 9 on p24, or a full layout, as figure 10. The following are some activities using large apparatus to explore body shape:

- Find different ways to hang/balance in curled or stretched shapes.
- From the same support position curl, then stretch high/wide.
- Support your body using both floor and apparatus in curled/stretched position or in a twisted shape.
- Repeat above three activities focusing on symmetrical/assymetrical shapes.
- Jump/drop from a low height in a stretched position, land in a controlled, curled position (bend knees and hips) to stand and stretch.
- Come off apparatus slowly using different safe landings, into curled and stretched positions.
- Spring/climb on to apparatus curled/stretched.
- Move over/up and down/along/under/around apparatus in curled/ stretched/symmetrical shapes.
- Move along/across/around your apparatus alternating between curled and stretched shapes; symmetrical or assymetrical shapes.
- Hang or balance, upside down, near the floor (using floor for support); can you change your shape in this position (l)?
  - Move freely on your apparatus; freeze in shape on teacher's command: 'curled, stretched, twisted', etc.
  - Make a sequence joining three different hang/balance positions: in the same place; then from three different levels on the apparatus.
  - Make a sequence using floor, mat and apparatus to involve a) curled, stretched, twisted shapes; b)symmetrical/assymetrical shapes; c) movements that are a combination of these shapes.

(l)

Conclusion

After the apparatus has been moved, practise the following activities to bring a lesson on body shape to a calm and relaxed ending:

- Practise any shapes you have made today. Can you join two or three together with a roll?
- Think of a mathematical shape or one you can see around you and imitate that shape.
- Make a bridge or machine shape.
- Hold a position of balance; keep varying your body shape.

(m)   (parts high)

Many of these tasks and activities can be adapted for use with partner work, eg moving together/apart; or sequence work, eg lifting different parts high (tummy, knees, feet, bottom, etc (m).

Remember to maintain the variety and challenge of activities by asking children to vary the **level**, **speed**, **direction**, and **strength/lightness** of movements.

Balance and supporting body weight

Supporting the body weight means holding the body still, using different parts of the body as a base on which to balance, primarily hands and feet. Children should investigate taking their weight on large body parts (patches) such as back, bottom, side, hips and front, as well as on small body parts (points), such as hands, feet, knees, and head. Ways of balancing and taking the weight of the body should include hanging and supporting the body, incorporating gripping apparatus from below or from the side. Children should experiment with moving into and out of balances, and learn how to incorporate balancing with a partner and in sequences of movements.

Introduction and warm up

The following are some warm-up activities to prepare the body for balance and support activities:

- Walking/running/jumping, and stopping on different parts of the body as suggested by the teacher.
- Practise different ways of running on the spot.
- Non-stop series of movements changing points of contact with the floor, eg feet, hands, knees, bottom.
- Move in different directions on hands or feet or other body parts.
- Running on the spot, jogging/knees high/with tuck jumps.
- Follow a partner to match movements: running, hopping, skipping, jumping, etc.
- Walk, jog or run while moving lower to the floor; roll to knees or feet, rise and carry on walking.

- Practise different patterns of jumping to end in different positions of support (different parts of the body, then freeze in a balanced body shape).
- Stretching activities (see p77).
- Class games/activities (see p43).
- Years 5 and 6: excercise circuit (see p77–78).

Floorwork

The following are some floorwork activities that explore balance and supporting body weight:

- Stretch high, then lower body slowly to sit/kneel/lie down on various parts of the body.
- Balance on any part of the body; be still for a count of ... seconds.
- Balance on a broad part of the body (patch) (n).
- Balance on small parts of the body (points) (o).
- Set challenges, eg: balance on one patch and two points; one point and two patches, etc (p).

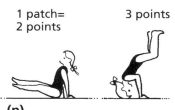

1 patch= 3 points   1 point
2 points

(p)

- Practise a balance at different levels or with different leg shapes.
- Take your weight on shoulders/hips/tummy/bottom; vary the shape.
- Take your weight on the hands and feet/head/elbows/knees; vary the level and shape.
- Balance on different points with body parts held high: tummy/bottom/feet/knees.
- Make different bridge shapes on different parts of the body (patches and points).
- Find different ways to support your body so that your feet are high.
- Balance, roll to second balance. Vary balances and rolls.
- Take weight on hands, bounce up bent legs from crouch position (bunny hops).
- Take weight on hands, then kick up legs behind (kicking donkey).

1   2

(q)

- Put your hands on the floor, walk feet up walls or wallbars (q).

Handstands

Try to do a free handstand with or without partner support (as appropriate). Coach for safety and correctness in doing a handstand, guiding children as follows:

1. Your hands on the floor should be a shoulder-width apart.
2. Keep your arms and body straight (like rods of steel!).
3. Move your hands forward on to the floor (r).
4. Throw your hips (and legs) up, above your shoulders, keeping legs straight.

(r)

Practices for the handstand should be repeated, and can lead to trying a headstand.

(s)

Headstands

Try to do a headstand (on a mat) with or without partner support (as appropriate). Coach for safety and correctness in doing a headstand, guiding the children as follows:

1. Use your head and hands to form a triangular base (s).
2. Place your head forward, taking your weight on the front of your head.
3. Walk your feet up slowly to a tuck position, keeping legs straight.
4. Hold your tucked position in balance.
5. Keep your back and legs straight as you kick up (try kicking one leg first).

Practice with a partner. If this is too difficult, begin by practising in a tuck position with bent knees.

Small apparatus

Extend the above tasks by using small apparatus (such as beanbags, hoops and ropes) as an object to reach; an object to avoid; or an object used as a point of contact for a given part of the body.

Large apparatus

The following are some activities using large apparatus that explore balance and supporting body weight:

With benches, mats, table and box tops

• Find different ways to balance and take weight on the bench, using patches, points or a combination of the two.
• Try different ways to balance using floor and bench for support as above (t).

• Balance on a bench or box top, roll to the floor and finish in a different balanced shape.
• Link two balance shapes with a step or a jump on/off the bench.
• Roll across a mat, make a balanced shape using the bench and floor, and return with a different roll on the mat.

(t)

• Join a jump, a roll and a balanced shape using the bench, the box top and mat.

With varied apparatus

Using figure 9 or figure 10 (see p24):

• Climb on the apparatus slowly; find a space to grip tight and be still; return to the floor slowly.
• Repeat the above, but move to a new position of support.
• Get on the apparatus forwards, backwards or sideways using different parts of your body. Dismount a) slowly; b) quickly.
• Find a position where you can hang or balance. Vary the shape you make.

(u)

- Hang or balance, supported by floor and apparatus.
- Hang or balance on apparatus on hands and feet and other body parts (u).
- Hang or balance with body parts high: tummy, feet, bottom, knees, etc.
- Find different ways to be upside down on apparatus, or on floor and apparatus.
- Link a floor and apparatus balance with a hang/balance on apparatus.
- All children in spaces on apparatus; teacher calls tasks for all to attempt, eg: hang/balance on hands and feet; one hand and one foot; one patch and one point, etc.
- Make a sequence of hangs and balances using a) apparatus, b) floor and apparatus; vary levels, shapes, direction and speed of linking movements, such as steps, climbs, jumps, rolls, turns.

Conclusion

After apparatus has been moved, practise the following activities to bring a lesson on balance and support of body weight to a calm and relaxed ending:

(i)

(ii)

(iii)

(v)

- Practise a chosen floor balance. Show good start and finish positions.
- Curl up in tuck position; stretch out to balance on various points (v i–iii).
- Practise three different ways to take weight on hands.
- Balance, roll and balance.
- Start in high stretch position, lower body slowly to a variety of finishing positions of support and balance.

Transferring weight

The transference of weight is achieved when the supporting part of the body is changed, such as in walking or running; and when the supporting base remains the same, as in jumping, hopping, sliding or rocking. Children should experience activities performed in a small space and on the spot, for example rolling, rocking, circling, turning, twisting, pivoting, lifting, lowering, jumping, springing, and swinging.

Introduction and warm up

The following are some warm-up activities that explore transferring body weight:

- Practise varied ways of moving on your feet.
- Find ways to jump and land: on the spot; on the move (be still when landing).

- Move in different directions on hands and feet or other body parts.
- Practise jumping and springing up on the spot.
- As above, varying shape/height of bounce.
- As above, twisting body in air to quarter, half and full turn.
- Run, jump and land (hips and knees bent for deep landing).
- Walk/jog/run in different directions, stopping in your own time.

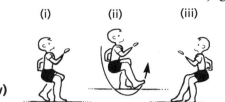

(i)   (ii)   (iii)

(w)

- As above, but practise pivoting when you stop. Carry on, moving in a new direction (w i–iii).
- Any combination of the movements of running, jumping, landing, pivoting.
- Follow a partner in any of these activities.
- Use flexibility, stretching and mobility exercises on p77.
- Use warm-up games and activities on p43.
- Use exercise circuit activities on p77–78.

Floorwork

The following are some floorwork activities that explore transferring body weight:

(x)

(y)

- On the spot. Take weight on different parts of the body.
  - As above, but vary shape from curl to stretch.
  - Practise different rocking movements in curled/stretched positions (x).
  - Practise rolling your body forwards/backwards/sideways.
  - Practise rocking and rolling into a balance position.
- Balance into a roll (y).
- Practise a variety of rolls, ending in different finishing positions.
- Stretch high, lower and rock on body to balance curled/stretched.
- Practise different rolls with a different starting position.
- As above, twist and lower body to a balance position.
- Balance in a stretch shape, curl and rock into new stretch balance.
- Find different ways to transfer weight from hands to feet.
- Weight on hands, kick up legs to bring down in different places (kicking donkeys), knees bent or straight.
- Take weight on hands, curled/stretched.
- Cartwheel (it may be appropriate to coach this activity for some children): face forward, lean forward, raise leading leg, lower and push, hands and feet contact floor in straight line, arms and body straight, look at floor, first landing foot close to hands.
- Find two or three ways to balance and link with rocking and rolling movements.

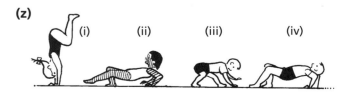

(z)

(i)   (ii)   (iii)   (iv)

- Find different ways to turn and rotate your body using: large body parts (patches); small body parts (points) eg, hands and feet.
- Find ways to pivot around a fixed point of your body (eg hands, head, foot) (z i–iv).

- Link two balances with a) a turn; b) a pivot.
- Fix a part of your body to the floor; twist body to touch floor at different points and with different parts.
- Find different ways to jump, land and then roll.
- Find different ways to roll and then jump.
- Link three different rolls with jumps and turns.

Small apparatus

Many of the previous floor activities can be given added interest with the use of small apparatus (eg, hoops, ropes, beanbags) as: objects to move into/around/over; and points of contact (especially useful for pivoting and twisting movements).

Large apparatus

The following are some activities using large apparatus, that explore balance and supporting body weight:

(aa)

Benches, box tops, low tables, mats

- Jump from the bench in a variety of ways, landing deep, then stand and stretch.
- As above, but follow with a roll.
- Move along/across bench, touching it with as many body parts as possible (aa).
- Move along bench using hands and feet a) forwards; b) backwards; c) zigzag.
  - Starting from different positions, roll on to mat from bench.
  - Roll from mat to finish on bench/box top (bb).
  - Roll along the bench.
  - Balance, roll, balance using a) bench and mat; b) bench only.

(bb)

Variety of apparatus

- Move on the apparatus, continuously touching it with various body parts.
- Move on the apparatus, continuously touching it with hands and feet only.
- Find ways to: a) move up; b) move down your apparatus, slowly.
- Hang and balance, move into a new support position, then to a different space to make the same shape.
- Find different ways to get on and off the apparatus from one point, then from various points.
- Find places on flat surfaces where you can slide, push and pull your body.
- Spring on to the apparatus forwards, backwards, sideways; dismount slowly, hands first.

(cc)

(dd)

- Roll along/on to/from the apparatus.
- Spring on to apparatus; roll along or off (cc).
- Roll to apparatus, jump on, hold balance and jump off with a deep landing.
- Move from apparatus: a) using hands and feet; b) springing from hands to feet.
- Move over apparatus using: a) hands and feet; b) hands and other body parts.
- Move over apparatus, using hands only, before landing on feet (dd).
- Move over, around, through apparatus, trying not to touch the floor.
- Make a sequence on the apparatus showing three hangs/balances.
- Find ways to lift, climb, then lower your body back to the floor.
- Make a sequence involving a jump, a roll and hands and feet movement.
- Make a sequence involving a spring, a circling/turning movement and a roll.
- Find places to swing your body (use of bars/ropes/wall bars is essential for this).

Conclusion

The following activities can bring a lesson on transfer of weight to a calm and relaxed ending:

- Practise a balance into a roll, and perfect it.
- Practise a roll into a balance, and perfect it.
- Find three or more positions of support using hands and feet only.
- Find three or more positions of support using other body parts.
- Balance on one foot in stretched position, tuck and lower body to floor in various end positions, then relax.
- Balance in curled shape, open out to stretch high and wide.

Remember to aim for quality in all movements, and to vary speed, level, direction, and force (lightness and heaviness).

Linking movements and sequences

'After a while it's like my body tells me what to do'
(primary child practising a sequence of movements)

In linking movements together, the aim should be for continuity, thus encouraging children to build up sequences both on and off the apparatus. The emphasis in teaching should be on smooth, continuous joining of movements; a good linking sequence should have a natural flow and could include rocking (to and fro), rolling (circular movement), pivoting (on a point, eg toes), turning, jumping, and stepping. It is a good idea to build up from simple sequences of two actions, but whatever the sequence, it should have a definite start and finish position. Encourage children to experiment, to think before they move, and to discuss the experience afterwards. Questions to ask include: What did they intend to do? Did the movements link well? Could they improve on the sequence? How?

Introduction and warm up

The following are some warm-up activities that explore linking movements:

- Run in different ways and directions all over the space; stop on signal.
- Walk, then roll and continue walking.
- Keep changing ways of moving on your feet: walking, running, hopping, jumping, skipping: a) in own time; b) on signal.
- Move on the spot continuously using your feet: a) jumping; b) in a variety of ways.
- Make a pattern of jumps: a) on the spot; b) on the move.
- Shake all body parts continuously to loosen up.
- Run: a) in different directions; b) back and forwards across the hall; on signal touch the floor with both hands and continue running.
- Keep extending/stretching your body in positions of balance.
- Keep extending and curling in positions of balance; vary levels.
- Practise a variety of linking movements.
- Use flexibility, mobility stretching exercises (see p77).
- Use warm-up games and activities (see p43).
- Use exercise circuit (see pp77–78).

Apparatus

The following are some activities using apparatus that explore linking movements:

Beams, benches, box tops, tables and mats

Using a four-inch low beam or an upturned bench:

- Jump on, then off the apparatus, land, and roll on a mat.
- Roll on a mat to the apparatus, step on it, jump off and roll on a mat (ee).
- Run, jump on the apparatus and spring off: a) with a deep landing; b) with a twist in the air.

(ee)

- Practise walking forwards and backwards on the apparatus.
- Practise walking along the apparatus, then pivoting on two feet/one foot and jumping off.
- Move on to apparatus, leave the apparatus using hands and feet, then roll on mat.
- Travel along the apparatus using jump, roll, or sliding movements.
- Travel along the apparatus, slide off the end and roll across a mat (ff).
- Roll on mat to apparatus, move along in various ways and jump off with deep landing.

(ff)

(gg)

- Make a balance shape on the apparatus, move to floor, roll, and repeat the balance shape (gg).
  - Make a jump on a bench and land in a balance shape, jump to floor and repeat the shape.
  - Make a sequence of rolls, turns, jumps and balances, staying on the bench.

Varied apparatus

- Move on and off the apparatus in continuous movements, in different ways: a) in one place; b) in various places.
- Jump from the apparatus, and roll to different finishing positions of balance.
- Make a sequence of a jump, roll and balance movements; repeat the sequence.
- Link two or three movements together smoothly on the apparatus only.
- Move to apparatus, move continuously on the apparatus and back to the floor.

(hh)

  - Repeat a swinging and rhythmical movement on the apparatus, land on the mat with: a) roll; b) hands to feet movement (hh).
  - Join a run, jump, spring over apparatus: a) along straight pathway; b) changing direction.
- Move to, over and away from apparatus with rolls and jumps, taking weight on hands and feet.
- Move around the hall from one piece of apparatus to another: a) touching floor in between; b) without touching floor.
- Link two pieces of apparatus together with a sequence to include: a) balances/hangs, rolls and hands-to-feet movements; b) turning, pivoting, rolls and balances; c) free choice.

Conclusion

After the apparatus has been moved, the following activities can bring a lesson on linking movements to a calm and relaxed end:

- Move smoothly from a balance to a roll.
- Move smoothly from a roll to a balance.
- Repeat a floor sequence you enjoy.
- Have a quiet, controlled class game or activity (see p43).
- Stretch, and relax completely on the floor.

Partner and group work

Partner work is best introduced in Years 5 and 6, when the children have developed a number of basic gymnastic skills. In developing partner work children should focus on:

High/jump

Low/crawl

(ii)

Follow with contrasting movements

(jj)

- Following a partner (to repeat movements).
- Mirroring a partner (following, facing or side by side).
- Contrasting a partner's movements (either following, facing, or beside a partner) (ii).
- Avoiding a partner (one forms an obstacle in a support or balance position, and partner moves over, under, or around, without touching).
- Supporting a partner (both balancing, taking partner's weight, moving together in contact) (jj).

Some of these activities will require partners to be of similar heights and weights; others work just as well with partners of contrasting body build. Children may have a special partner with whom they work well, but they should experience working with a variety of partners during the year. The value of partner work lies not just in moving together, but in the opportunities it gives for close observation of each other, and discussion about what they have done or intend to do. Working with a partner often gives confidence to less able children.

Introduction and warm up

The following are some warm-up activities that involve working with a partner:

- Follow a partner about the hall: a) running; b) jumping; c) use other movements.
- Running freely; on signal run into groups of two, three, four or more.
- In pairs. Play a partner game (see p43).
- In pairs. Hold hands, find ways to move about together.
- In pairs. Join together with other body parts, eg legs, arms, hands, feet; find other ways to move.
- In pairs. Run backwards and forwards across the space (keep a record of how many times you cross in a given time).
- Use stretching and mobilising activities (p77).
- Use exercise circuit (p77–78).

Floorwork

The following are some activities that involve floorwork in pairs:

- Find a way of making a balancing shape with two bodies that partners can achieve together.
- Watch, and copy your partner's slow actions: a) facing each other; b) side by side; c) back to back.
- Perform one movement slowly, and synchronise the movements with your partner: a) facing each other; b) side by side; c) back to back (kk).
- Perform a balance shape with your partner, first of matching, then of contrasting shapes and/or levels: a) facing each other; b) side by side.
- As above, but add another balance shape, then add a roll to the sequence.

(kk)

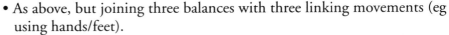

(ll)

- As above, but joining three balances with three linking movements (eg using hands/feet).
- Find ways to pass over/around/under your partner's balance position.
- As above, but: a) matching with; b) contrasting with partner's balance.
- Move over each other's balance position, alternating balances and movements in turn.
- Support your partner in various positions of balance, using hands and body as a means of support (ll).
- Each partner finds balances which can counterbalance the other (mm).

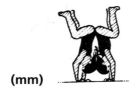

(mm)

Group work in three or fours

Any of the above tasks can be attempted in small groups, for example by:

(nn)

- Following each other to mirror movements.
- Moving together and apart in twos: a) matching; b) contrasting.
- Assisting in balances (eg one supporting two or three children) (nn).
- Assisted flight or spring movements.

Apparatus (varied)

The following are some activities using apparatus for paired or group work:

In pairs

(oo)

- Follow your partner on/off the apparatus with: a) matching actions; b) contrasting actions.
  - From opposite directions mirror partner's actions on to and off apparatus (oo).
  - Side by side, synchronise actions moving towards/along/ over/round apparatus, and again when moving away.
  - Show identical and contrasting balances on the apparatus, or identical and contrasting ways of moving away and finishing.
- Balance/hang so that both of you are in contact in different ways.
- Balance on floor and apparatus so that partner can move over/through shape (pp)
- Combine any of the above tasks to make a pair sequence.

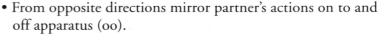

In groups of four to six

(pp)

- Find different ways for all to be active at once, working co-operatively and safely.
- Work in pairs or threes to follow or face each other in contrasting and matching movements and balances.
- Plan and perform a group sequence using floor and apparatus.

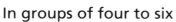

Conclusion

- Practise with a partner a balance or sequence from earlier in the lesson.
- Class games (see opposite) can be used either as an introductory or ending activity.

Games activities

The following games involve vigorous cardio-respiratory activity and stretching activities. They are ideal for use at the start of a lesson as an introductory warm-up activity, or at the end of the lesson to make an active ending to a lesson (followed perhaps by all lying on the floor, like 'dead lions' completely quiet and relaxed).

Tag
- **Free tag:** several chasers, wearing bands, tag others who join the chasers. After one minute count the number left. Start again with new chasers
- **Pair tag:** a pair chase with their hands joined. Those players who are caught join hands. When there are four together, divide into pairs and so on.
- **Change tag:** a pair chase; the touched player replaces the tagger (several pairs can chase).
- **Chain tag:** two or three chasers; tagged players join hands with the chaser (maximum six to eight). Restart game when this number is achieved.
- **Stuck in the mud:** two to four chasers. Tagged players stand still with legs apart. They can be released by free players by: a) touch; b) crawling through legs.

Traffic lights
Children respond to colours (eg coloured cards shown by the teacher) by movement:

Red – stop. Perform task or balance suggested by teacher.
Amber – get ready, in crouch position, for the next colour.
Green – hopping, jumping, running, etc on command, in different directions or at different speeds.

Compass
Children run/move in variety of ways to compass points in the hall at the command of the teacher, eg 'North/South/East/West'. For fun, false pointing could accompany the command. Various body challenges can be suggested at each compass point. Increase number of commands to NE, SE, SW, etc at later stages.

Lifeboats
Played like Compass, but children have to memorise nautical terms for areas to run to (eg, lifeboats (run north), quarterdecks (south), overboard (east), giant wave (west + holding partner), sharks (lines at centre), submarine (lie flat!) Captain (stand and salute). This can be substituted by any class topic, adapting names/actions as appropriate.

Numbers

Children run freely, teacher calls numbers. Children join hands or sit back to back in the appropriate group size. Class is timed by how long it takes for all to be ready. Substitute skipping, jumping, hands and feet movements; numbers in other languages or answers to simple mental arithmetic.

Bridges

In pairs. Partner A makes a body bridge. Partner B passes over or under as many times as possible in a set time (20–30 seconds). Change over.

Straddles

A stands with legs apart. B passes under and around legs as many times as possible in a set time (20–30 seconds). Change over.

Turn the turtle

A lies flat on tummy, pressing down hard. B tries to turn A over, remembering to bend the knees, and keep the back straight.

Stubborn donkey

A on all fours, hands, knees and head up. B tries to move donkey by clasping both hands behind neck, bending knees and pulling back. As an alternative, B can try to push the donkey over.

Draw numbers (or names, letters, shapes)

Children outline numbers with points of the body when in support positions. For example, lying on back or shoulders, draw a number 48 with one foot, or both feet together.

Beanbags

One bag each. Use as a point of contact for hands or feet: a) reach points of the compass; b) be the hands of a clock. Both provide good maths links.

Team relays

In fours and threes. With a time limit; running, jumping, hopping across the hall in shuttle. Set the best team score.

Over/under

One playball per pair, one metre apart, with feet fixed. A stretches back overhead, ball in both hands, to B, who hands the ball back through A's legs. After six 'over/unders' they change roles.

For Resources for gymnastics see p184.
For Assessment of gymnastics see pp168, 170.

Dance

'When I dance I feel my whole body come alive' *(primary child)*

Dance is an art form known to all cultures. It can be used to communicate ideas, feelings and stories, through rhythms and patterns of movement that are both disciplined and spontaneous. Children should experience many kinds of dance, including creative dance, traditional folk dance, historical dances and popular modern dances. Many curriculum activities can be enriched by the use of dance and movement; dance can contribute to a child's physical development, rhythmic sense and aesthetic awareness. Through dance children can enjoy physical experience and gain a satisfaction not to be found in any other activity.

Dance has become an essential part of physical education in the primary school. In the past, many teachers of older primary children have not felt the need to teach dance on a regular basis, but those who do find it stimulating and rewarding for the children, and for themselves. Dance is a medium that all can enjoy, including the disabled. It can awaken and help develop our kinaesthetic sense, and many popular forms such as disco dancing can be a useful health-related exercise. Children can be helped to understand that dance is both athletic and expressive, demanding a high level of fitness, and can itself help develop body control, strength and mobility.

As teachers, we need to build on the natural, free movements of children, to help them create, perform and appreciate a wide range of dance movements. The following suggestions are aimed at helping you develop a programme for dance for primary years 3 to 6.

This section on dance provides a guide to:
- What to teach
- Lesson planning
- Movement ideas
- Dance themes

What to teach
dance in the National Curriculum

'Dance is a distinct art form, with its own history, body of knowledge, aesthetic values, cultural contexts and artistic products. It offers a variety of learning opportunities and enables participants to enjoy physical experience as well as develop intellectual sensibilities.

(National Curriculum Physical Education Interim Report, 1991)

The Programme of Study for dance at Key Stage 2 says that pupils should:

- make dances with clear beginnings, middles and ends involving improving, exploring, selecting and refining content and sometimes incorporating work from other aspects of the curriculum, in particular music, art and drama;
- be given opportunities to increase the range of body actions, including step patterns and use of body parts;
- be guided to enrich their movements by varying size, shape, direction, level, speed, tension and continuity;
- in response to a range of stimuli, express feelings, moods and ideas and create simple characters and narratives in movement;
- describe and interpret the different elements of a dance.

A programme for dance should include units of work and activities which focus on:

THE BODY	BODY ACTIONS
• Different parts supporting weight and leading actions. • Increasing flexibility and tension. • Correct posture and shape.	• Gesture. • Bending and stretching. • Inclining and leaning. • Momentum and continuity.

ACTIONS IN SPACE	STIMULI
• Forming pathways by skipping, stepping, leaping, springing, rolling.	• Expressing feelings, moods, ideas in response to music, poetry, story, painting, artefacts, festivals, worship.

RELATIONSHIPS	DYNAMICS
• With partners, groups, individuals, audience.	• Explore rhythms with use of body sounds and percussion to form dance patterns.

Dance movement

Dance is important in helping to provide a balanced programme of PE activities, especially those which develop aesthetic qualities and the artistic expression of moods, feelings and ideas. In dance, as in other PE activities, children should be helped to **Plan:** discuss and compose; **Perform:** practise and improve; **Review:** describe and appreciate.

While the emphasis will be on performance, planning and reviewing should continue to be developed during Years 3 – 6. By observing and describing the movement of other children or dance professionals, they can begin to analyse and appreciate their own actions and those of others. In observing, reviewing and evaluating, dance elements to consider include:

What is moving?
What body parts?
(eg arms, legs, hands, whole body)

What action?
In place and travelling
(eg twisting, lowering, skipping, stepping)

Dance movement

Where are you moving?
In what directions?
(eg up, down, forward, backwards, sideways, diagonally)

How do you move?
What speed and quality?
(eg quickly, slowly, smoothly, heavily, lightly)

What relationships are formed?
What links are made between individual body parts, partners, or groups?

The forms of dance

Dance can be divided into two categories:

Creative dance

Creative dance involves exploring, creating, practising and improving dance movements that are linked to a stimulus, idea or feeling. Stimulus for creative movement can be found in music, art, English, history, geography, religious education, and other subjects in the curriculum. By responding to a variety of stimuli, children can explore and improvise, then select and practise their movements, and finally form them into dance sequences and routines.

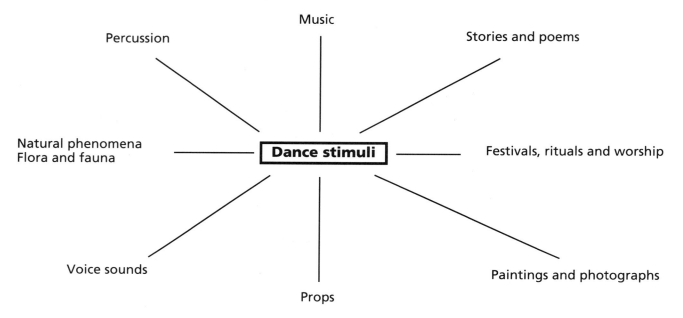

Percussion

Music

Stories and poems

Natural phenomena
Flora and fauna

Dance stimuli

Festivals, rituals and worship

Voice sounds

Props

Paintings and photographs

Folk dance

Folk dances are dance forms from different times and places, and are linked to a cultural context; for example, English Morris or clog dances, Asian dances, or African dances.

The ideas and suggestions in this chapter deal mainly with creative dance, but a section at the end includes folk dance, with steps and examples of dances from British and European traditions.

Percussion

In addition to handclaps percussion instruments such as drums, cymbals, gongs, claves, bells, maracas are all useful for strong rhythmic movements when tapped or banged, and for soft, smooth, flowing movements when scraped or smoothed. The tambourine is very popular because it offers a wide variety of sounds to stimulate a broad range of movements, and is easy to use whilst on the move. Children can experiment at playing instruments in a variety of ways: shaking, striking, tapping, scraping, smoothing using fingers, palms and backs of hands, and using different beaters as a stimulus to create their own dance movements.

Music

Various forms of music can be used as a stimulus to develop children's movement, although they need to be chosen carefully, and a good quality sound system is essential if children are to respond to the music sensitively and creatively. The music needs to have a distinct mood or simple rhythm, and variety in tempo, rhythm or volume. Children can be asked to move to its rhythms and moods, or they can move using the music as a background for their actions. For suggestions for dance music see Resources for dance (pp185–6).

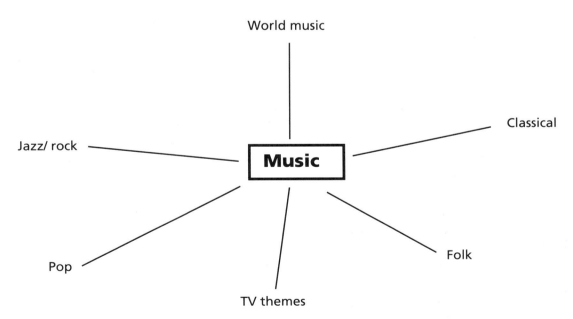

Stories and poems

The words and rhythms of poetry can inspire exciting dance ideas, while stories, through their themes and characters, can inspire sensitive responses to relationships, as well as exciting rhythmic actions.

Stories can provide a stimulus for creating a dance/drama to represent a narrative theme, character or idea. Traditional literature such as religious stories, Greek myths or the works of Shakespeare (eg the witches' dance in *Macbeth*) can provide a good source of stimulation for older children. Most children enjoy fantasy themes such as monsters, space, ghosts, robots and so on. Poetry sources can include narrative and theme poems as well as poems with a strong rhythmic beat.

Festivals, ritual and worship

Religious customs, celebrations, stories and rituals from different faiths are a rich source of ideas for dance, and allow children to learn about other cultural traditions and beliefs. Music and worship will often underpin religious celebrations where the themes of praise, thankfulness, sacrifice, prayer, petition, joy and sorrow can develop into whole body actions, including leaping, stepping, skipping, bowing, bending, kneeling, and gestures with hands, face and arms.

Language and voice

Words can be used as a stimulus for bodily action; children can be asked to match movement to the meaning of a given action word, such as 'punch', 'dodge', 'spin', 'slither' or 'explode'. The voice can be exaggerated and used dramatically to heighten mood or action, or it can take on the movement itself and become an onomatopoeic expression. Children can be encouraged to create patterns of movement from a sequence of words such as 'crouch, rush, pounce' or 'flutter, whirl, fall'. The following are some words for action that can be used as a stimulus for dance:

walk	stop	bang	slide	duck	twist	reach
jog	freeze	clap	push	dive	turn	spread
run	hold	slap	pull	fall	spin	grow
stride	settle	stamp	glide	flop	whirl	rise
hop	hide	shake	rush	crumple	twirl	ascend
skip	hover	hit	dodge	pounce	swing	tower
jump	pause	crash	feint	grab	sway	explode
leap	look	throw	fly	clasp	stretch	explore
crawl	listen	cut	dash	cling	arch	escape
roll	wait	tear	drift	respond	close	scatter
spring	balance	rap	dart	shrink	open	climb
	still					
	lie					
	sit					
	crouch					
	kneel					
	stand					

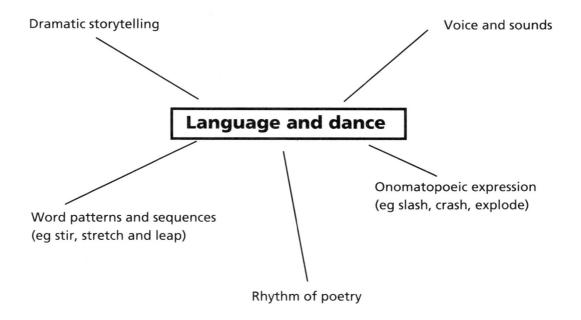

Dramatic storytelling

Voice and sounds

Language and dance

Word patterns and sequences
(eg stir, stretch and leap)

Onomatopoeic expression
(eg slash, crash, explode)

Rhythm of poetry

Props

Props and artefacts can be used to heighten dance movement and to interpret it. Children enjoy holding ribbons, streamers and scarves which can be waved and swirled. Their movements can be copied by a partner or used to enhance dance movements. Props such as chairs, hoops, ropes, chalked shapes, can take on a variety of meanings for dance drama.

Natural phenomena, flora and fauna

The movements of animals, the growth of trees and plants, and observation of the nature of fire, wind and water, storms, hurricanes, volcanoes, etc can provide rich and varied stimuli for dance.

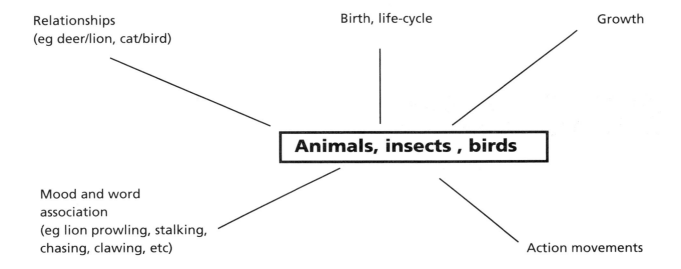

Relationships
(eg deer/lion, cat/bird)

Birth, life-cycle

Growth

Animals, insects , birds

Mood and word
association
(eg lion prowling, stalking,
chasing, clawing, etc)

Action movements

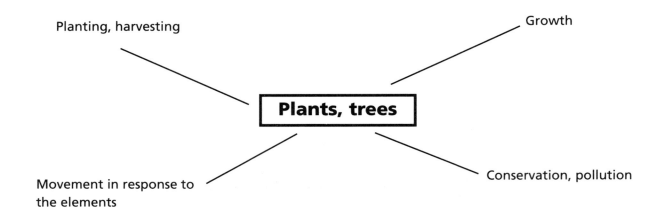

Planting, harvesting

Growth

Plants, trees

Movement in response to the elements

Conservation, pollution

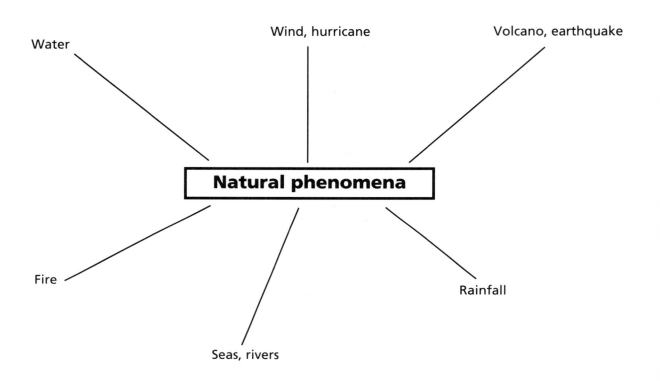

Water

Wind, hurricane

Volcano, earthquake

Natural phenomena

Fire

Rainfall

Seas, rivers

Lesson planning

Lesson plans may include:

Introduction and warm up (2–3 minutes)
Introductory discussion, tune-in, building up confidence and concentration, with movements in unison; body awareness, sensing and stretching; travelling over all the area.

Movement exploration and development (8–12 minutes)
Practise varieties of movement, vocabulary and skills, individually, in pairs or as a group.

Dance theme (10–12 minutes)
Creating a dance, selecting ideas from stimulus and theme, developing it into an individual, pair or group dance.

Conclusion (3–4 minutes)
Quiet warming-down activity, a time for reflection, review and evaluation.

Points to remember before the lesson include:
• Plan carefully, building on what children have done.
• Link to cross-curricular work wherever appropriate.
• Tune-in the children to the lesson (planning and motivation).
• Prepare music and other resources beforehand.
• Keep a memo card of planned activities.
• Children change appropriately – PE clothing and bare feet if possible.
• Are you changed appropriately and ready to move and join in when necessary?

Introduction and warm up

Ensure that the children are mentally and physically tuned in – listening and ready to move – before you begin. It is often a good idea to direct the activities with use of percussion, using a clear stop and listen signal. Children can be asked to find their own space before you start, and sit down. Begin with simple movements in unison to give confidence, with attention focused on the teacher. Move from sitting, kneeling or crouching on the spot, to moving in confined space (with a radius of two to three metres) and then to travelling around the hall. Warm up with specific exercises, allowing for differentiated responses to include bending, stretching, twisting, turning and swinging body exercises. Also encourage travelling freely and rhythmically around the hall, finding spaces, without touching other children.

Warm-up activities

• Walk, leap, step, jump to steady tambourine beat, all over the hall.
• Move freely in one place to shake different body parts to the rhythm of a tambourine.
• Combine two of the above activities in a sequence.

- Call out various action words (see p50) for children to move to (repeat the words as necessary) eg 'walk, walk and leap and leap', 'skip, skip, skip and jump'.
- Contrast relaxed and extended body positions, eg feet apart, stretch legs wide in standing position, reach back arms over head then lean forward and let top half of body flop forward (hang loose) and repeat.
- Practise being floppy and hanging down from sitting, kneeling, lying positions.

Moving and breathing
- Lie on your back, listen to your breathing.
- Feel what body parts help you to breathe (breathe deeply down to your toes!).
- Curl up (breathe in) now stretch wide (breathe out).
- Think of other ways to prepare for action (breathe in) and move (breathe out).

Exercises on the spot
- **Head:** prop and lift; forward and back/side to side; rotate fully left and right; circle in both directions (draw a circle with your nose).
- **Shoulders:** lift and drop, circling, shrugging, pressing back.
- **Arms:** swing and rotate arms rhythmically; forward, backward, across body; arms bent, stretch elbows up and back and rotate freely.
- **Spine:** weight on hands and knees; curve, stretch, bend and wriggle your back; lie on your back, tuck up and stretch (repeat on left and right sides); lie on your back with your feet over beyond your head; practise rocking in sitting position; practise rolling forward and backwards.
- **Legs:** sit and reach to touch outstretched ankles/feet/toes; stand and hang loose, reach to touch floor in front and between feet (legs straight).
- **Hands:** stretch fingers wide; clench the fists hard; shake them loose.

- **Feet:** lying on back; wriggle your toes, curl and extend them; rotate and extend your ankles.
- **Face:** exercise it with contorted stretches, using the five vowel sounds: 'a e i o u'.

Body massage
Rub, press and loosen muscles in arms, neck, legs and joints to:
- Warm and prepare body for action.
- Increase body sensing.
- Increase awareness of body parts and vocabulary.

Body balance sequence
Using percussion as stimulus:
- Find different ways to stretch and balance at different levels.
- From standing, practise ways to kneel, sit, lie, crouch and stand again (practise at various speeds: six beats, four beats, two beats, etc).

- As before, but start from low position on different body parts.
- Find ways to roll (three or four beats) then stretch (one beat).
- In standing position, clap high, clap low, clap high, clap to left and to right; make up a sequence.
- Standing and stretching in all directions (up, down, left, right, forward and back): call out directions to set rhythm; choose directions and repetitions to set rhythm; children choose and make own rhythms with percussion.
- Make skipping sequences on the spot, springing from one foot to the other (a hoop or shape on the floor is useful to step in and out of).
- Jumping sequences: two feet to one foot (and vice versa); crouch to star jump; tuck jumps (to touch knees in the air); with twists in the air.

Pathways and travel

Using lively, rhythmical music or tambour:
- Find various ways to run, then stop different body parts, then stretch and continue.
- Practise hopping, skipping and galloping as above.
- Leap and land on one/two feet; stretch arms/legs in balance.
- Stepping/marching/strutting in different directions (find different ways to walk and step).

In all of these travelling activities emphasise use of space, no touching, exploring space around you and moving in relation to others.

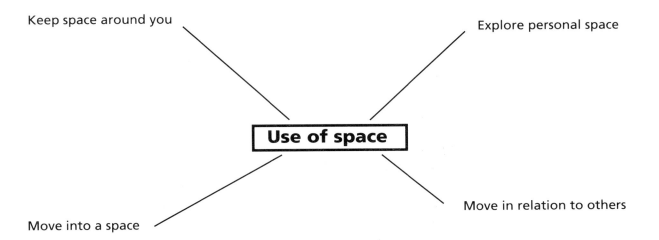

Movement ideas

exploration and development

The main movement ideas selected for each lesson should be explored and developed in a variety of ways using repetition and contrast. The basic elements of movement include body parts, body moves, body steps and body shapes – all will be needed for exploring movement.

Body moves

Body moves include stretching and bending, twisting and circling, lifting and falling, swinging, swaying and shaking; there are many ways of categorising body parts and body moves and it is useful to list those with which you intend to work in your programme plan. The following are examples of basic body moves:

Head
- Hold head high, stretch neck up; how tall can you stand?
- Stand straight, bend head forward, tuck chin in; can you see your toes?
- Bend head back; can you see the ceiling above you?
- Nod (say yes with your head), and shake head (say no). Fast and slow.
- Move head from side to side, back side to side and forward side to side.
- Move head round and round. Copy teacher's or partner's head moves.
- What parts of your head can you move? Raise eyebrows, wink/blink, wrinkle nose, smile please (say 'cheese'), open mouth wide, bare your teeth, puff out cheeks (blow), wiggle your ears!

Trunk
- Bend at the waist, touch your toes, crouch low, curl into a ball, roll over.
- Bend at the waist and lean back – what can you see behind you?
- Twist your upper body, left and right; keep feet still!
- Hands on hips and swing those hips from side to side!
- Stick out tummies, bottoms or chests.
- Shake all over, fast and slow.

Arms
- Raise your arms and reach up high, reach for the sky!
- Touch your head, and shoulders, knees and toes.
- Swing your arms round and round, forwards and backwards, see how fast!
- Reach out wide, move arms up and down by your side; like a bird fly high and low.
- Swim with your arms, on the spot; swim fast/swim slow.
- Shake your arms up, shake them down, shake those arms all over the town!
- Flop forwards with arms swinging (like an ape!) and move round the room.

Fingers and hands

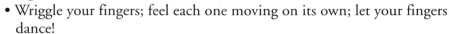

- Wriggle your fingers; feel each one moving on its own; let your fingers dance!
- Clap hands loudly, then very softly; clap in the air, clap the floor; have a happy, clappy time!
- Rub your hands till they feel warm, and shake them from the wrists (fast/slow, high/low).
- Use your fingertips to do a skipping dance around you on the floor.
- Let your fingers skip around your body and in the air all around you – above, below, in front, behind, side to side, far and near, etc.

Legs

- Put your left/right leg out and shake it all about!
- Lift a leg, kick a leg, kick it high, kick it low, kick it fast, kick it slow!
- Keep your leg straight: how high can you lift it? Left leg? Right leg?
- Lift one leg back and bend forward, arms out wide, can you balance? On each leg?
- Feet apart. Knock your knees, bend them wide, move them out and in; flap your legs.
- Wobble your legs, wibble-wobble jelly-legs!
- Lift leg sideways, right and left; one after the other, as quick as you can.

Feet and toes

- Stand on tiptoes, right foot and left foot.
- Wriggle your toes, wriggle each toe (are they all there?).
- Lift your foot, bend your foot up and down, side to side, round and round.
- Touch the floor with your heel then toe, heel/toe; change feet (heel/toe).
- Do a foot dance! A rain dance! A sun dance! A special day dance!

Body steps

We can use our feet rhythmically and spatially in eight basic steps. These step actions move the body from one place to another. They are:

- Walk: a transfer from one foot to the other on the ground.
- Run: a transfer from one foot to the other off the ground.
- Leap: a running step from one foot to the other.
- Jump: taking off and landing on both feet.
- Hop: taking off and landing on the same foot.
- Skip: a step hop, changing legs, with an uneven beat.
- Gallop: a run with an uneven beat.
- Slide: a walk with an uneven beat, lead foot sliding.

These steps can be organised in sequences, for example:
• Walk, leading to run and leap.
• Jump, leading to hop and skip.
• Gallop, leading to slide.

The following are some activities to help explore and develop co-ordination in body steps.

Marching (to music or drum)
• Find a space, march on the spot, lift knees, hold head high.
• March on the spot to given rhythm ('left, right', 'one, two'); swing arms in time with legs.
• Walk around marching to music or drumbeats (no one must touch!).
• Walk and swing arms high.
• Walk and lift legs high.

Walking and running
• Walk or run – freeze on given signal (look at the 'statues': Are they strong? Do they move?).
• Skip/hop/jog/jump; encourage children to change direction and stop on given signal.
• Fast/slow; accelerate or decelerate on given signal.
• High/low; walk or run high or low (near to ground) on given signal.
• Walk or run then jump (stretch), land and stop quite still.

Combining steps
• Walk, leading to run.
• Walk, leading to run and leap.
• Walk/run, changing to hopping.
• Jumping, leading to hopping, changing to skipping.
• Children create their own walk/run/jump/hop/skip dance to music or given beat.

Galloping and sliding
• Children gallop, as if they were horses, not touching each other.
• A gallop, slowing to a slide, slowly stopping.
• Children gallop/slide in pairs, holding hands.
• Children gallop/slide in pairs, one after the other (then change leader).
• A group of children gallop/slide in line, weaving patterns of movement.

Body shapes

Every body has a shape, even when it is not moving. We can all create body designs in space, designs that are still (shapes), and designs that move (dancing shapes). The following activities explore and develop awareness of variety in body shape. Make the shape and hold it as still as you can. See what shapes you can make.

Irregular shapes ('crooked man' movements)

- Make 'crooked' fingers: bend fingers (use both joints, both hands), clench/unclench hands.
- Twist the hands, bend wrists backwards and forwards, inwards and outwards. Use sharp, quick movements. Hold until given signal, eg on castanets.
- Bend elbows out, up and down; do an elbow dance.
- Move head forwards, sideways, backwards, etc. On given signal change your head!
- Bend trunk (from the waist), bend knees and ankles; knock your knees, twist your feet.
- Stand still; stick out one part of your crooked body, eg hip, on given signal.
- Walk in your crooked shape, stop on signal and change shape!

Regular shapes (tall/small, wide/narrow)

- Start in a small shape (like a seed); slowly rise until body has grown tall and stretched high.
- Move slowly/quickly from tall, to small and narrow.
- Move from small to wide, then to tall and wide (really stretch out!).
- Change your shape and size; at given signal, hold it. Can you make a circular/round shape?
- Walk your shape and size; change at given signal. Are you in good shape?

Try dividing the class in half, into tall and small shapes, to make a dance. Tall/wide people move into the centre and make a circle. Small/narrow people move through the tall/wide people's legs, then turn and move out again.

Circles

- Draw circles in the air with one finger, using finger joints.
- Draw circles with all fingers, using wrist joints.
- Draw large circles with whole arm, using shoulder joint.
- Do the above, using both hands.
- Put hands together (palms touching) and make large circles in the air.

Drawing shapes

(Initially, it is a good idea for the children to copy the gestures of the teacher.)

- Draw a shape in the air with your finger, eg letters, numbers, simple geometrical shapes.
- Draw the shape with the whole hand (moving wrist/elbow joint).
- Draw the shape using the whole arm (moving elbow/shoulder joint).
- Draw the shape using both hands/arms (and by putting both hands together).
- Make a dance with your hands in the air (hands meeting and turning around each other, fingers wriggling or pointing).

Changing shapes

- Sit on the floor. Notice your body is making a shape. Your shape is different from the next person's. On three, I want you to sit in another shape: one, two, three. Good; now find another shape. One, two, three...
- Make some more strange shapes: a bent shape (bend arms, legs, whole body); a stretched shape (include fingers and toes); a twisted shape; a round shape.
- Make a shape you have never seen before.
- Make a shape standing on one leg.
- Move around in your shape without touching anybody. When you hear the signal, change shape.

Exploring movement

All movement involves space –moving in one's own space and moving in the space shared by others. Even when a person is not moving, their body is making a **shape** in space, at a certain **level**. When a body moves it has **direction, size, place, focus** and **pathway**; all these elements can help to extend and explore any kind of movement, and can be summarised as:

- Shape: body design in space.
- Level: low, medium and high levels of space.
- Direction: forwards, backwards, sideways.
- Size: big, little.
- Place: on the spot; moving through space to another place.
- Focus: direction of gaze.
- Pathway: straight, curved, circular, zigzag, etc.

Movements can be characterised by different kinds of **force**. Words used to describe the force of the movement can be first introduced and demonstrated by the teacher. Later, children should be able to use the vocabulary themselves to describe what they have done. Examples of ways of describing force are soft, light, strong, heavy, sharp, jerky, smooth, and sustained. All movements can be altered by changes of force. For instance, movements can be sharp or smooth, strong or light. They can be held in tension, or be loose and free-flowing.

Movements also vary in time. They have a **rhythm**, an underlying beat or pulse, that can be decided by teacher or child. They always have a **speed** (fast or slow), and a **duration** (long or short). We need to help children explore contrasts in all these elements, and help them describe what they have done.

Children need to develop the language of dance. One way of describing movement is through imagery, which can be a wonderful stimulus for dance: 'Show me a flower growing ... a wild horse galloping ... a branch swaying in the wind', but it can also be a limiting factor. Children readily get 'in role', and see dance as a form of play. The danger in using imagery is that children focus on trying to be, for example, a prowling cat, rather than on the kinds of movement they use to describe being like a cat. A good way to introduce and to explore movement is through interpreting the imagery present in poems, stories or ideas.

The following offer some possibilities for helping children to explore movement. A stimulus can come from artefacts, songs, poems, music or stories. Children will have their own ideas of what their movements are like. All these ideas can be developed through writing, drawing, topic work or story-telling.

- Soft, light movement: like flying balloons, hopping birds, fluttering butterflies, floating feathers, flickering candles, falling leaves, drifting snowflakes, etc.
- Strong, heavy movement: like a person lifting a heavy weight, a bear, a bulldozer, a carthorse, chopping wood, digging a hole, an elephant, a moon-walker, etc.
- Sharp, jerky movement: like busy bees, machines, mechanical toys, puppets, robots, sparklers, woodpeckers, etc.
- Smooth, sustained movement: like a cat prowling, fish swimming, cream being poured from a jug, a glider, things growing, ice melting, the sun rising/setting, skaters, etc.
- Movement which grows bigger and collapses: like a balloon inflating/deflating, breathing, candle flame rising/snuffed out, flowers unfolding/wilting, snowman being built and melting, etc.
- Moving up and down: like hands (conducting music), kites, water, planes, bouncing ball, roller coaster, yo-yo, etc.
- Moving back and forth, across or around: back and forth like bells ringing, lions in a cage, pistons, sweeping leaves, rowing a boat, a rocking horse, swings, trees in a breeze; around like curling smoke, a record, a revolving door, a roundabout, a washing machine, a wheel, a windmill, etc.
- Moving high: like climbing a ladder/mountain, clouds, high-flying birds, kites, a plane taking off, skyscraper, stilt-walker, tallest tree, etc.
- Moving low: like a bird skimming the water, hunter in the woods, a landing plane, minibeast, snake, diving turtle, etc.
- Moving fast: like an arrow, ambulance/fire engine/police car in an emergency, bullet, racing car, cheetah or antelope, etc.
- Moving slow: like a baby crawling, a broken-down car, flowers growing, old people, a slow-moving river, slow music, etc.

The key to engaging children at all ages is variety. Try to include the unusual, the interesting challenge. Value the differences in children. They must all work within their capabilities, and the sign of growth is doing something new and something different. By combining actions through repetition and contrast we begin to form a sequence – and a dance is created. Lessons may have the following stages of development:

Introduction ⟶	**Movement training** ⟶	**Dance theme**
(Presentation and focus on key movements.)	(Exploration of movements, building into a sequence.)	(Movements linked into a simple dance.)

Dance themes

Dance themes can be presented in a variety of ways, including:

- **Teacher and class:** moving near and far from the teacher is helpful in early experiences when confidence needs building.
- **Individual:** useful for all levels of experience, where children make up their own sequences and dances from teacher stimulus, or their own exploration/stimulus, eg using percussion.
- **Pair dances:** moving in unison or opposition to each other, for example: beginning and ending together; moving in relation to partner (up and down, towards and away, over and under); with some body contact with partner; reacting to partner's words/feelings (observe each other carefully).
- **Follow the leader:** in file, copying a set pattern (in pairs or groups), changing leaders frequently; groups either in line or with leader at front, facing class (as teacher); movements can be matched or contrasted.
- **Circle dance:** leader can be in the middle and group can copy or respond. Ensure a secure structure for inexperienced dancers; move in a circle, forward and back, either across the circle, or by changing places with a partner.
- **Group dance** (for more experienced children): keep movements simple; move in file, in line, in a circle or freely; move to change shape of group: come together, draw apart; interact and respond to movement of other groups.
- **Half-class dance:** group A play percussion while group B dance (and vice versa); group A observe/evaluate while group B dance; group A are statues or move on the spot while group B dance.
- **Dance patterns:** each dance sequence can be given a letter to be repeated as appropriate, eg: A = moonshine (glowing/contrasting/palling); B = sunset/sunrise (lifting, spreading, life-giving, heating, fading, setting); C = stretching/rising; D = chasing/playing. The pattern of movement could vary A B C B, B C D B. The following are some themes that can be adapted and developed for dance:

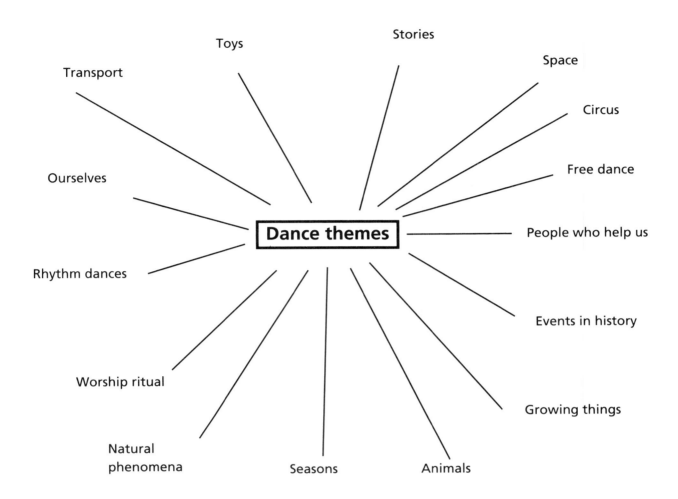

Here are some examples of ways of developing these dance themes:

Events in history
Many events in history can be represented through dance/drama. This is an example of a dance theme taken from the study of the Second World War.

Effects of war
Create dance movements and sequences from some of these elements:

- Bombs exploding; rockets firing; planes climbing/banking/diving; parachutes floating.
- People running, hiding, falling, sheltering, praying, frightened, sad, shocked, injured, dying.
- Wardens/firefighters, climbing, saving, dragging, digging, lifting, lowering.
- Building shelters; screwing, lifting, hauling, banging, bolting, piling sandbags.
- Homes: shapes of wrecks; shattered, broken, hanging, flattened, blazing.

- Soldiers: marching, running, jumping; contrast with crawling, dragging, maimed, returning, celebrating.
- Familes: waiting, worried, sad/happy, separation/reunion, supporting, helping.
- Peace: joy, celebration, greeting, reunion, forgiveness, unity, hope.

Story

Dance/drama can be used to express a story or narrative. This example is based on the common theme of escape, and can be linked to the previous theme of the Second World War and prisoner-of-war camps.

Escape

- Prisoners: sad, bewildered, fearful, hungry, starving, isolated, crowded.
- Guards: marching, running, beating.
- Escape: lowering, tunnelling, crawling, sliding, lifting, hauling, creeping, hiding, motionless; contrast with running, jumping, leaping, dodging.
- Pairs: lifting, carrying, lowering, parting/meeting.

Natural phenomena

Many examples of natural phenomena, drawn from the study of nature, science or geography, can be used as themes for dance. Here is one example:

Volcanoes and earthquakes

Create dance movements and sequences from some of the following elements:

- Earth's crust: rocks (symmetrical/assymetrical), layered, smooth, spikey.
- Surface: sea, shore, land, mountain, desert, forest, river shapes.
- Earth's plates: moving, sliding, folding, rising, falling.
- Earth's core: core/inner core. Contrast liquid rock with granite and metals.
- Magma: thick, sticky, pushing, covering, sliding, rippling.
- Lava; flowing, slowing, hardening.
- Ash: flying, falling, covering.

- Effects of disaster: homes blazing/flattened; countryside scorched/covered; people frightened/homeless.

Water

- Rain: falling, whirling, splashing, spraying; contrast drizzle/storm, light/heavy.
- Rainbow: arch-shapes, sun/rain contrasts.
- Storm: rain cascading, flooding, drowning, whirling.
- Rivers: contrast stream/river, trickling/flowing, crashing/meandering, waterfalls/whirlpools; slowing, drying, stagnating, bubbling, tumbling.

- River activities: sailing (sails billowing/flapping), rowing, canoeing, punting.
- Sea: contrast waves rising/falling, rolling/crashing, sinking/floating; foaming, spraying, tossing.

Wind
- Trees: bending, swaying, leaning, rocking.
- Leaves: swirling, falling, scattering, floating.
- People: contrast frightened/elated/refreshed; leaning, walking, falling, jumping.
- Whirlwind: contrast flattening/lifting; crashing, whirling, spiralling, spinning.
- Birds: soaring, diving, hovering, swooping.
- Sails: billowing, flapping, hanging, filling.

Birds
- Movement and shape: in flight/on land; use arms, legs, whole body to underline contrasts of different birds: swans, swallows, eagles, sparrows, etc.

Space
Outer space
Create dance movements and sequences from some of these elements:
- Dust and gas: whirling, circling, colliding, merging, solidifying.
- Particles: breaking, flying, scattering, floating, shooting.
- Meteorites: contrast symmetry/assymetry, curved/spikey, smooth/pointed.
- Stars: exploding, spinning, propelling, circling, forming, sucking (black holes).
- Sun: light, heat, flares.
- Planets: circling, orbiting, spinning, pathways.
- Comets: trails, pathways, flaming, burning, crashing.
- Contrasting planets: Pluto (tiny, frozen); Uranus (icy, green); Saturn (dust rings); Jupiter (giant, gaseous); Mars or Neptune (rocky, hot); Venus (hot, bright); Mercury (tiny, rocky, hot); Earth (life-giving, water, colour, beauty).

Space exploration

- Astronauts: parting, leaving, excitement, worry, space-suits; walking, stepping, climbing.
- Lift-off: motors exploding, firing; rocket lifting, tilting.
- Space travel: contrast gravity pulling/holding/weightlessness; rolling, turning, twisting, floating.
- Robots: contrast smooth/jerky; maintenance of spacecraft.
- Landing: lowering/upthrust, spinning, turning.

- Exploration: weightless walking, jumping, leaping, measuring, collecting, digging (slow motion).
- Return: engine fire/misfire; panic, fear/courage; pair help/support; return/re-entry; tension, joy, celebration, reunion, praise.

Worship, festivals, ritual
Worship
Bodily actions could include bowing, bending, kneeling, prostrating; moving smoothly from one to the other. Prayer could be expressed through:
- Kneeling: use of upper body, arms and hands in confession/forgiveness; offering/receiving, asking/ thanking, blessing.
- Standing: use of whole body as above; include lifting/lowering actions.

Festivals and celebrations
These could include creation, harvest, New Year, spring, etc, as well as religious events such as Passover, Chinese New Year, Diwali, Easter, Ramadan, etc. Celebration could be expressed through free dancing, leaping, joining with others in patterns and sequences of movement.

Ritual
Ritual movements could be linked with processions: walking with poise, precision and pride; in twos, fours, eights; in line, abreast or in files.

Dance games
These can be used at any time, but are especially useful at the beginning of a lesson:
- **Move and freeze:** move freely, and freeze when tambour/music stops: feet off the ground (balancing on different body parts); or balance on one/two/three/four/five points of the body; or balance to lift body parts high (as called by teacher).
- **Musical statues:** freeze in geometric/animal/colour/action shapes when music stops. Vary it with pairs in contrasting shapes.
- **Tag:** half the class freeze in statues, spread about the hall. While music plays, the other half imagine they are being chased and avoid capture by dodging, swerving, ducking, stopping. When the music stops, children freeze and reverse roles (variation: to avoid being caught, the stationary group can duck, dip, sway, crouch on the spot).

- **Musical games:** in pairs. Children mime to TV theme music, eg *Match of the Day:* passing and catching, bowling and batting, kicking and saving; contrast movements – react to partner's movements. Freeze in action shapes when music stops.
- **Dancing feet:** follow partner's jumping/step patterns. When the music stops, balance in similar or contrasting shapes.

- **Pairs:** children step/skip/leap freely. When the music stops they freeze and face the nearest partner to mirror action, contrast action, show different ways of greeting (no touching). Different partner each time.
- **Clapping rhythm games** (see *Active PE* Book 1 (pp59–60)).

Folk dance

Folk dance gives children the opportunity to increase the range and complexity of body actions, in step patterns and use of body parts. It is:
- fun;
- provides healthy exercise;
- improves body skills and co-ordination;
- provides social awareness and contact.

Steps and simple dances

The aim of these notes is to help you to teach children dance steps and simple folk dances; create dance patterns; and to move rhythmically to folk, traditional, and contemporary music with a steady beat and rhythm.

Walk and skip

- Walking/stepping to the rhythm: six, eight or twelve steps in various directions.
- Walk/skip on the spot to six, eight or twelve beats.
- Repeat the above with a partner.
- Repeat, and vary with skipping steps.
- **Dance:** in pairs, side by side, six steps on the spot; join hands, walk forwards six steps and backwards six steps, drop hands; six steps on the spot.

Slip-step and skip

- Practise slip-step to left and right to beat of eight (one foot moves sideways to be joined by the other).
- Repeat the above, holding hands with a partner.
- Practise slip-steps freely, increasing spring and speed of steps.
- **Dance:** hold hands in a circle; six slip steps to the right, 12 skip steps to the left; drop hands, six skips on the spot; join hands and repeat with 12 steps to the right and six steps to the left.

Meeting and turning

- Skip/step freely to the music. On signal, face nearest partner.
- Touch palms (shoulder high) one/two hands and move away.
- Step on spot to beat of six, touch palms, move away.
- Link arms at inner elbow, turn once; practise right and left arms.
- Step on spot to beat of six, link right arms, turn twice right, link left arms, turn twice left, move away and repeat.

- Face a partner, four steps apart, walk two steps forward. Link right arms, turn twice and step backwards to original position. Repeat with left arms.
- **Dance:** in pairs (boy/girl), form two circles, one inside the other; face partner, two paces away; step forward, link arms, turn to right, step backwards to starting place. Step forward, link arms, turn to left, step backwards to starting place. Inner circle joins hands, walks six paces left. Outer circle joins hands, walk six paces right. Drop hands, face new partner and repeat. Vary by introducing skipping and side-stepping.

Do-se-Do

- Skip/step freely to the music in different directions.
- Add rhythmic stamps (on the spot) to beat of four or six.
- As above, stamping forwards, backwards, sideways.
- In pairs, practise do-se-do without music, then with music.
- Face partner, four steps apart; take two steps forward, one step sideways and two steps back, passing around your partner.
- Practise do-se-do walking/skipping.
- **Dance:** face partner, four steps apart; stamps on the spot four times; walk forward, clap palms (shoulder height), step back twice; walk forward, do-se-do to right, step back; walk forward, do-se-do to left, step back; walk forward, link arms to turn to the right and to the left and return to place; four rhythmic stamps on the spot; and repeat. Vary by skipping or clapping instead of stamping on the spot.

Turning two hands

- Standing side by side, practise cross-arm link to hold partner's hands.
- Practise stepping/skipping in different directions.
- Face partner, four steps apart.
- Step forward, cross-link hands, turn to left and return to place.
- Step forward, cross-link hands, turn to right and return to place.
- **Dance:** (first without music, then with music) form two circles – girls inner circle, boys outer circle – face partner; step to partner, cross hands, turn to right, turn to left and return to place; inner circle join hands, skip right, only stopping when facing partner again (while boys clap to beat); step forward, two right turns, and two left turns with partner; outer circle join hands, skip left until facing partner (girls clap to beat); step forward, two right turns, two left turns; both circles rotate simultaneously in opposite directions; when back to original positions, repeat the whole dance.

Turning one hand

- Practise one-hand turn, right hands joined, shoulder height; palms forward, fingers pointing upwards, elbows bent.

- Turn to right, turn to left, using same procedure with left hand. Skip with partner side by side freely about the hall.
- On signal, skip on the spot facing partner, four steps apart.
- Skip forward, right-hand turn twice; skip backwards to place.
- Skip forward, left-hand turn twice; skip backwards to place.
- **Dance** (a reel): in four to six pairs in sets about the hall; face partner, four paces apart (ie, one line of boys, one line of girls); lines step forward, touch palms (or nod/bow) and step back; lines step forward, right-hand turn, left-hand turn and step back; lines step forward, do-se-do and step back; end pair join hands and slip-step between lines and back to their places; end boy and girl peel off and lead their lines to the far end; here they join hands to make an arch for all to link and pass under; all move along one place leaving the 'arch' pair at the far end of the set. Repeat until all pairs have completed the sequence (Figure 12).

Fig 12: Turning one-hand dance

```
B      B      B      B
                           ARCH
G      G      G      G
```

Star reel

- Practise star turns: two boys, two girls facing each other; hold hands at centre as for one-hand turn; circle right, walking; repeat circling left; repeat to beat of the music (Figure 13).

Fig 13: Star reel dance

```
        B        B

        G        G
```

Dance: in sets of four pairs about the hall; each set in two lines (boys and girls), holding hands, facing each other; skip forward, nod/touch palms and back; skip forward, right hand-turn with partner and back; skip forward, left-hand turn with partner and back; four in centre perform right-hand star turn, then left-hand star turn; outside couples perform two-hand turns to right, then left; end couple join hands, skip to far end of set, between the lines. Repeat dance sequence until all couples have completed the circuit.

With these basic steps and formations as a background, children will be ready for more varied dances which can be found in *English Folk Dancing in the Primary School* (Novello, 1960).

Assessment

Record of achievement

A suggested list of criteria for recording achievement in dance could include:

1. Range of body actions and dance movements.
2. Form, line and control.
3. Expressive quality.
4. Creative/innovative movement.
5. Planning actions and dances.
6. Ability to describe and evaluate.

For more on Assessment in dance see p168.

Resources for dance

Dance equipment could include:
- A robust, good-quality record/cassette player or midi system.
- Small cassette players for flexible class use.
- A variety of tuned and untuned percussion instruments, eg tambourine, drum, triangle, chime bars, castanets, coconut shells, cymbals, maracas, shakers and children's class-made instruments.
- A range of tapes, CDs or discs for dance, including examples from pop, rock, soul, jazz, TV themes and BBC sound effects, as well as collections of music from other cultures.

For more Resources for dance see pp185–186.
For more on dance themes see Book 1.

Games

'It should be noted that children at play are not playing about; their games should be seen as their most serious-minded activity'
(Montaigne, 1533–1592)

As part of our national heritage and the heritage that we share with all peoples and cultures, games will become a major feature in the recreational lives of our children, and should, therefore, feature as an essential part of any PE programme. Games offer children a wide range of educational experience: the development of physical skills; exploring the tactics and principles of play; and the fostering of personal qualities through sporting co-operation and competition.

Research shows that skills, understanding and attitudes develop best, and gender differences are less marked, when all children have access to a structured programme of games teaching. Children are better motivated and their performance increases in quality when assisted by an adult in active learning. This section aims to help you create your own structured programme of games teaching, and is divided into:

- What to teach – games in the National Curriculum.
- Lesson planning.
- Warm-up activities.
- Skills development.

What to teach
games in the National Curriculum

'A balanced games programme should also contribute towards a pupil's social and cognitive development by providing opportunities for co-operation, competition, problem-solving and decision-making.'
(PE for ages 5–16, DES, 1991)

The Statements of Attainment at the end of Key Stage 2 say that pupils should be able to:
- plan, practise, improve and remember more complex sequences of movement;
- perform effectively in activities requiring quick decision-making;
- respond safely, alone and with others, to challenging tasks, taking account of levels of skill and understanding;
- evaluate how well they and others perform and behave against criteria suggested by the teacher and suggest ways of improving performance;
- sustain energetic activity over appropriate periods of time in a range of physical activities and understand the effects of exercise on the body.

The Programme of Study for games can be summarised as follows:

Fig 14

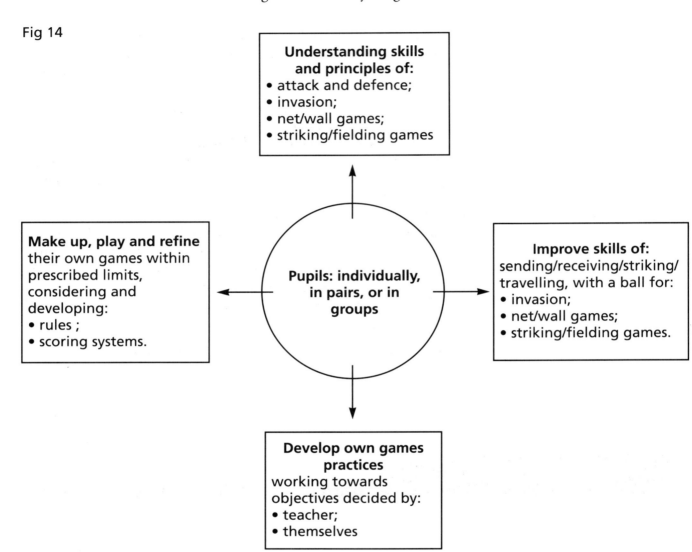

Understanding skills and principles of:
- attack and defence;
- invasion;
- net/wall games;
- striking/fielding games

Make up, play and refine their own games within prescribed limits, considering and developing:
- rules ;
- scoring systems.

Pupils: individually, in pairs, or in groups

Improve skills of: sending/receiving/striking/travelling, with a ball for:
- invasion;
- net/wall games;
- striking/fielding games.

Develop own games practices working towards objectives decided by:
- teacher;
- themselves

The following units of work aim to cover the Attainment Targets and Programmes of Study outlined above:

Footwork turning running jumping hopping skipping landing stopping	Awareness of space/others chasing dodging avoiding principles of attack and defence	Ball skills hand-eye co-ordination foot-eye co-ordination stopping, passing kicking, throwing hitting, catching bowling, fielding travelling with the ball

Game skills defending attacking shooting blocking tackling	Games invented games invasion games striking/fielding games net/wall games

Three kinds of game should be experienced at Key Stage 2:
- **Invasion games:** such as football, mini-rugby, mini-hockey, netball/basketball.
- **Striking/fielding games:** such as cricket, rounders, softball, stoolball.
- **Net/wall games:** such as tennis, volleyball, mini-badminton.

Each group of games has common principles of play, but will differ in detail according to the game being played. In the primary years, children should experience games from all three categories and be shown the common principles of play. They will, for example, need constant practice with a variety of bats and balls, to build skill and competence. Many of our national games, such as cricket, football, hockey and rugby are technically demanding for many primary children, so it is necessary to modify games to allow all children to participate actively and successfully.

Small apparatus for use in these games should include balls of various size and texture, hoops, ropes, quoits, bats of varying types and size, mini-hoc sticks, and short tennis racquets (See Resources p186).

Lesson planning

Assuming a 30-minute, active games session, a typical lesson plan might take this form:

Warm up ⟶ Skills development ⟶ Games activity ⟶ Ending

- **Warm up** (5–6 mins): energetic, heart-related activity to involve stretching, jogging, running, jumping, skipping. This may be game-related and involve the whole class (and the teacher!).
- **Skills development** (5–10 mins): use a variety of games equipment so that children learn to experiment with their movements and games

Fig 15: An example of a grid for skills development - rugby skills (See p91 for more on rugby skills.)

apparatus. This could involve the whole class working individually or in pairs at the same activity (good when starting a new skill). Half the class could practice the same activity with the teacher, while the other half work independently in pairs or small groups at known skills and practices. The whole class could work in small groups at different activities (in grids or stations), with teacher focus on one group experiencing a new activity (see figure 15).

Running/carrying ball (Rugby skills)
(size of grid to vary according to need)

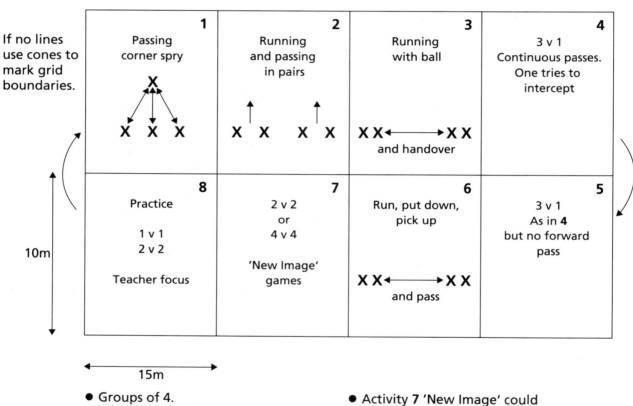

If no lines use cones to mark grid boundaries.

10m

15m

- Groups of 4.

- Rotate every 2/3 minutes.

- Activity 7 'New Image' could involve 2 groups (if 4 v 4) with one group moving on at every changeover.

- **Games activity** (6–12 mins): games can be created by the children or suggested by the teacher, and can be played individually, in pairs or in small teams. Use the skills to support the game, and the game to reinforce the skills. Ways of organising games activities include: dividing the class into small groups, practising/playing similar games; or dividing the class into small groups, practising/playing different games (groups to rotate once during the lesson and on a weekly basis. The teacher can focus on the new game to be learned).

Skipping	Netball	Football or Hockey	Rugby
For 60 secs. Count maximum.	Shooting. Best score from 20/30 attempts.	Dribble around cones.	Touch down and pick up.
Cricket Game	Fielding	'Count the catches'	Cricket Bowling
French Cricket Own bat and ball games.	Overarm throw in pairs.	Small ball corner spry.	In pairs.

Fig 16: Grid for practising a range of games skills

- **Ending** (3–4 mins): this may involve returning and tidying apparatus; reviewing and analysing skills and techniques; a warming-down activity.

An example of a games lesson

Year 3:   **Class size: 30**   **Autumn term**

Theme: Invasion games (ball footskills and body skills)
Lesson time: 30 minutes
Resources: size 4 playballs, cones

Warm up (5 mins)
- Free practice with balls near changing area (ball each).
- Walking/jogging to show change of speed/ direction: swerve, dodge, stop in 20m x 20m area.
- Stretching activities and vigorous whole-body jumping.

Skills development (10 mins)
Find different ways to do the following:
- Individual dribbling. Stop ball on signal (inside/sole of foot).
- Balance/rebound ball on different body parts (head, knee, chest, etc).
- In pairs, one ball between two. (A) dribbles ball to avoid touching others; partner (B) runs behind and becomes dribbler: a) on signal; b) at random.
- Find different ways to pass ball to partner: a) when stationary; b) on the move.

Games Activity (10 mins)
- Children in pairs. Invent a game using any skills practised during the lesson.
- Non-stop football: create a number of small goals around the perimeter of the playing area, using cones two metres apart. In 2 v 2 or 3 v 3, pass and dribble to score goals, aiming at a minimum of three to four passes between each goal attempt (see figure 17).

Ending (5 mins)
- Children return apparatus (all groups to be involved).
- Review the skills learned during the lesson (using question and answer).
- Ending activity: stretch high and wide, tuck low; repeat.

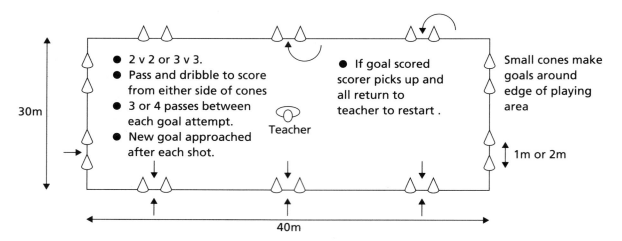

30m

40m

- 2 v 2 or 3 v 3.
- Pass and dribble to score from either side of cones
- 3 or 4 passes between each goal attempt.
- New goal approached after each shot.

Teacher

- If goal scored scorer picks up and all return to teacher to restart .

Small cones make goals around edge of playing area

1m or 2m

Fig 17: Non-stop football in small teams

Points to remember

- Change into tracksuit and trainers, setting a good example to the children.
- Note your lesson plan, eg carry a card in your watch strap, listing the planned activities.
- Disperse the equipment around the edges of the activity area for ease of access.
- Use brief instructions, and allow questions from children.
- Allow brief demonstrations by small groups of children.
- Review good effort and behaviour at the end of the lesson.
- Use walking to and from the lesson as part of the activity programme: encourage control, poise, spacing and consideration for others.

Warm-up activities

Each lesson should begin with warm-up activities to prepare children for the active games to come, and could include some basic warm-up activities (suitable for all PE lessons), mini-games, or small apparatus work, eg hoop activities. Choose from the list below to suit your children's needs

Basic warm-up activities

Walking, jogging, running

in different directions to show:
- Change of speed.
- Sudden stop.
- Swerving and sidestep.
- Forward, sideways and backwards movements.

Running

- Run in different directions, and stop. Return to starting place on signal.
- As above, adding jump, skip, hop, run on the spot.
- Stop on signal and crouch jump for 20/30/40 seconds (best personal score?).
- On signal, bend/crouch to touch ground with one/both hands; continue running.

- Stop on signal; crouch down, bending knees and hips, keeping centre of gravity low.
- As above, but pivot on one foot; rotate with short steps 20/30 degrees, then run off in the new direction.

Jumping

- Jump to make stretch or tuck shapes in a variety of ways.
- Jump with feet together and apart alternately; show different ways of doing this.
- Jump, as above, sychronising arms, together and apart – make up a movement sequence.
- Run, jump and reach high with one/both hands.
- Jump forwards, backwards and sideways; make different patterns of movement.
- Jump over/in and out of ropes, hoops or markings.
- Perform crouch jumps for a set time.
- Perform a standing long jump from a marking; measure the length in steps or spans.
- Take three or four steps to long jump; take off with one foot, land on both feet.
- Hop on one foot. On signal, hop on the other foot. Make up a sequence of hops.

Stretching activities

- Reach high with arms.
- From free-standing position, extend and bend arms back, arching shoulders and neck.
- Arms circling, bending and pressing back and swinging from side to side.
- Trunk turning, twisting, bending sideways, arching.
- Legs stretching (hamstring): stand with legs astride and straight, raise heels, extend and rotate each foot.
- Reach forward to touch floor; walk hands backwards.
- Balance on one leg; pull the other foot up behind bottom, then swing leg to kick up to alternate hands. Change legs.

Exercise circuits for years 5 and 6

Using simple strength, mobility and endurance exercises, set a maximum time (20 seconds is long enough to start with) during which children repeat each exercise. No apparatus is necessary. Emphasis should be on personal performance, improvement and quality of exercise (five good press-ups are more valuable than ten bad ones). See diagram for an example of an exercise circuit involving ten simple exercise activities.

Fig 18: Example of an exercise circuit

Exercises (four to six will be enough to start with) could include:

1 crouch jumps;
2 burpees (front support, squatting position, stand up);
3 astride jumping, with arms raised;
4 rope-skipping on the spot;
5 jumping back and forward over hoop;
6 press-ups (from knees to start with);
7 sit-ups (bent knees, feet flat, reach to knees);
8 squat thrusts;
9 dorsal raises (on tummy, raise legs, arms and chest together);
10 shuttle run x 5 metres (two parallel lines five metres apart; touch with alternate hands);
• others to be devised by children/teacher.

Mini-games

Mini-games, suitable to begin and end the lesson, for lower juniors, include:

Statues

Children walk, jog or skip in any direction. Teacher calls out a shape to make, eg elephant, goldfish, tree, etc. Children freeze in that shape. Teacher asks children to demonstrate the most creative, funniest, most still or most realistic shape.

Numbers

As above, but the teacher calls out a number; that number of children then join hands in circles. Variations can be calls of 2+2, 4-1, etc, or numbers in another language.

Shapes

The game is played as above, but children make a geometric shape with any parts of their body.

Freeze!

Children move like frogs, snakes, soldiers, giants, etc and freeze on teacher's command. Any movement is lightly observed and no dropping out is necessary.

Simon says

Children obey teacher's command or action only if prefixed by 'Simon says'. Children may have lives which are lost, rather than having to drop out.

Stuck in the mud

Two or three children are chosen as chasers and try to tag as many others as possible in a set time (eg one minute). If touched, children stand with legs wide apart. They can be released by touch, or, at a later stage, by a 'free' child crawling between their legs. No tagging while under legs.

Tag

- Tail tag: all children have braid (tails) in their shorts, and try to collect the tails of others.
- Pair tag: chaser tags children, who then join hands. When four are tagged, they break into two pairs and contnue tagging.
- Chain tag: as above, but groups hold hands to make chains up to five or six children long.

Basket full

Teacher scatters beanbags; children try to fill the basket by collecting as many of the beanbags as they can. As the children fill the basket, the teacher empties it. No one must carry more than one bag at a time.

Treasure hunt

Teacher calls a signal; the children search in all directions and then run to the appropriate corner (if North, South, East or West is called), make the shapes as required, make the actions ('digging' or 'climbing'); lie flat ('pirates'); stretch high ('treasure').

Pairs

Children run, skip or jump, without touching. On a signal, pairs of children either link arms, or hold hands, stand back to back, or make a pair bridge. There are no losers; any children left over join the teacher.

Circle trap

Half the class hold hands high in a circle (the 'trappers'); the remainder run in and out of the arches. On the call of 'trap!' those caught inside the circle join the trappers, ready for the next round.

Pass the parcels

The class forms a large circle. Between two and eight beanbags are given out (evenly spread between the children in the circle). On a signal, children pass the 'parcels' as quickly as they can in one direction (right or left). Nobody must be caught with two beanbags. The bags must be passed not thrown! Variety can be added by changing direction on signal.

Follow the leader

In small groups. The actions of the leader must be copied by the children, following in line. At first the teacher calls the actions; later, children can take the role of leaders of their group.

Shadow steps (to be played on a sunny day)

One child runs and swerves; their partner tries to step on the shadow of their head, arm or body. On a signal they change roles.

Jump the streams

The class – or half the class – jump over as many 'streams' (lines marked, or ropes laid out, on the ground) as possible in a set time.

Other warm-up activities can be found on p76.

There are many activities that may form part of the gymnastics lesson, but which can also be used as introductory games activities, such as these hoop activities :

Hoop activities

Big hoops are easier to move into, though smaller hoops can be handled and moved more readily. It is important that two or three sizes are available to cater for different ages and stages.

(a)

Movement with a static hoop

- Find different ways to move around/over/into/out of the hoop (a).
- Walk/jump/hop/run/skip between all the hoops in the activity area.
- Jump in and out of all the hoops (there should never be more than one in a hoop!).
- Find ways to jump into and out of your hoop (b).

(b)

- Can you slide into and out of your hoop? Roll into and out of your hoop?
- Use hands and feet to move into and out of the hoop.
- Run and jump into the middle of the hoop, landing on two feet.
- Step/jump into/out of a hoop held close to the ground, horizontally, by a partner. Find other ways to get over the rim without touching it.
- Step/jump through a hoop held vertically/diagonally.

Moving the hoop

(c)

- Show ways to move the hoop around/over you (c). No throwing in the air!
- Hold the hoop vertically, by your toes, on the ground. Step through, swing the hoop forward over your head and back to the ground.
- As above, backwards. How many can you do?
- The above can be speeded up until children are skipping.
- The same progression can be used with a two-foot jump.
- Skip the hoop on the spot/around the play area.
- Spin/twist the hoop around different body parts (waist, ankle, arm, etc).

Rolling the hoop

(d)

(Small/medium hoops are easier.)

- Roll the hoop in different ways along the ground; stay close to it (d).
- Using two hands, one on top to guide, one behind to push and rotate, set the hoop rolling.
- With a partner, three or four metres apart. Roll the hoop between you.
- Can the hoop be rolled/spun backwards?
- Spin the hoop, like a top, on the ground.
- While it is spinning, can you clap hands? Run round it? Other actions?
- Roll the hoop while walking/jogging/skipping. Stop on signal.

(e)

Games with hoops

- Horses: in pairs holding inside and outside hoop. Horse and rider run freely/run to touch set targets. Change roles on signal (e).
- Prisoners: in twos or threes inside hoop. Move together carefully in one direction; run to reach set targets; move over and under obstacles (f).
- Hoop relays: one hoop between four. Include passing the hoop, rolling while running, running through a hoop, and hopping or skipping. Relays can be there and back, or shuttle relays, with two children opposite each other, 10 – 20 m apart.

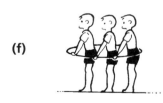

(f)

- Musical hoops: when music stops/on signal, run inside hoops. Teacher to call number of children. Hoops should be dispersed evenly about the games area.
- Frogs: in twos or threes with two hoops. Place second hoop so you can jump/step from hoop to hoop about the games area, or to a marked line and back again.
- In pairs or small teams. Invent your own game using one or two hoops.

Skills development

The activities in this section cover most of the basic skills that will help children to enjoy games. The skills developed are related to real games and provide a context in which children can practise their skills.

Invasion games

Invasion games include netball, basketball, football, rugby, hockey, etc. The following introductory skills are useful for all ball games, and should be practised with large or medium playballs.

(g)

Balancing/holding/carrying the ball
- Balance the ball on different parts of the body (g).
- Find different parts of the body to hold the ball: two ankles, knees, hand and shoulder.
- Hold the ball with two hands; stretch high/low/backwards/forwards with ball (h).
- Pick up the ball from various points around you.
- Roll the ball a few metres and pick up on the move.
- Run with the ball under one arm/in both hands/between two markers/zig-zag between cones.

(Rugby practice balls can be used for all the above activities.)

(h)

Passing and rolling the ball
- Throw with one/both hands; move to catch: a) with bounce; b) without bouncing.
- Find different ways to throw and catch your ball. How many times without dropping?
- Toss the ball high, above your head; cradle ball with arms and chest to catch (i).
- Roll the ball with your hands: a) in all directions, staying close to it; b) dribbling round cones.
- Roll the ball and pick it up on the move; bend your knees (j).
- Roll the ball to aim at wall/target/cone/partner's legs.

(All the above can be practised individually or with a partner.)

(i)

(j)

Bouncing the ball
- Drop/toss the ball from varying heights, to bounce and catch.
- Toss a ball overhead/sideways and catch on the move.
- Bounce and catch the ball while sitting/crouching/standing.
- Bounce and pat the ball: a) while stationary; b) while on the move; c) around cones.

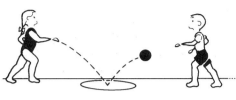

(k)

- Pat-bounce the ball (imagine it is on the end of a piece of elastic) with either hand, in different directions. Can you look up as you move?
- Throw and bounce the ball into a hoop for partner to catch (use push-pass: fingers behind ball) (k).
- Pass-bounce the ball to a partner, on the move, taking only one step holding the ball.

Passing, throwing and catching the ball

- Show different ways to throw and catch a ball when: a) stationary; b) on the move.
- Rebound the ball against a wall to catch: a) with a bounce; b) without a bounce.
- Throw the ball to aim at a wall target/low netball ring/hoop held by partner.
- Throw and catch the ball from a sitting/crouching/standing position: how many throws and catches in 20/30 seconds?
- Pass and catch the ball in pairs: a) while stationary; b) while on the move facing each other; c) sideways; then while walking, jogging (only one step allowed with the ball) (l).

(l)

Patting or hitting the ball (net games)

Use palm of hands to begin with; inner wrists and forearms can be tried later.

Individually (one light playball each):
- Find ways to pat the ball in the air with: a) one hand; b) both hands.
- Hit the ball up continuously; allow the ball to bounce between hits: hands palm-up like a tennis hit (m).

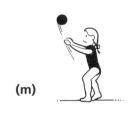

(m)

- As above, but without a bounce; now use fingers above head to push the ball up high: bend elbows, push, and flick the ball up.
- As above, push ball up continuously. Bend knees as well as elbows: try to get under the ball and push up. How many can you do?
- Try a combination of low hits, using palm and inner wrist, and high pushes, using fingers and flicking the wrists up.

All the above can be tried with a partner, hitting alternately or randomly. Now try the following exercises in pairs:
- Hit the ball up and over a line or rope for your partner to catch or hit/push back: start by clenching fist and hitting ball with inner wrist (serving to begin play) (n).
- As above, but continue to hit until play stops: a) with a bounce; b) without a bounce.
- In groups of three, four or five. Practise keeping ball up, by hitting and pushing up high – no one may make two consecutive hits: a) with a bounce; b) without a bounce.

(n)

• As above, with a rope 'net' 1.5 – 2 m high (3v3); keep the ball up (no scoring). Only three hits (maximum) for each team before ball is returned over 'net'. Encourage the use of two hands wherever possible.
• Invent a game using a ball and 'net' (eg high rope strung between two netball posts).
• As above, with 2v2, 3v3, 4v4, 5v5 children. Children can now make up rules for scoring, serving and restarting play.
Note: further refinements in play can be left to secondary school and Key Stage 3.

As confidence grows, challenge, co-operation and mild competition can be introduced for the previous activities, as follows:
• Personal best scores.
• Best score within set time limits (20–60 seconds).
• Best consecutive score.
• Best score while partner practises another timed skill.
• Co-operative scores in pairs or small teams.
• Small games, eg 1v1, 2v1, 3v1, 2v2.

Netball and basketball skills

These games involve the skills of sending and receiving the ball. They help develop hand/eye co-ordination, and are useful preparation for netball and basketball.

• **Target ball:** (1v1 or 2v2) defend targets (cones) from ball rolled or bounced from opposition. Children must keep behind a marked line when guarding or attacking (see figure 18).

Fig 18: Target ball

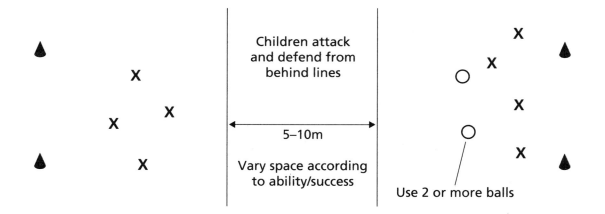

Children attack and defend from behind lines

5–10m

Vary space according to ability/success

Use 2 or more balls

• **Circle target ball:** (3v3, 4v4) no players are allowed inside a marked circle around the target (see figure 18a).

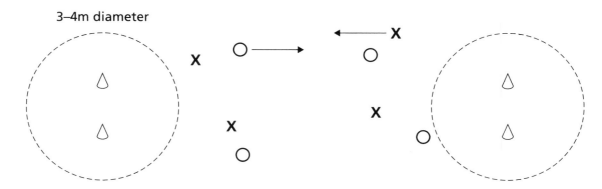

3–4m diameter

No players in circles.
Attack and defend cones (increase or decrease number of cones) according to ability.

Fig 18a: Circle target ball

Coach:
variety in passing to free (unmarked) players, eg over and underarm; running to space after pass to receive ball; keeping eyes on the ball; shielding ball by pivoting and screening with body; faking or feinting a pass to beat opponent.

• **Children's target game:** children invent a throwing/passing game involving targets and a ball. Discuss and demonstrate their rules and tactics.

• **Piggy in the middle** (variations). Build up from 2v1, 3v1, 2v2, 3v2, 3v3, 4v4 games: a) players aim to score five or ten consecutive passes without interception, or passer becomes piggy in the middle; b) aim for as many passes as possible within a set time (60 seconds). For both games, change possession or piggy on restart.

• **Passing relays:** divide class into four teams of six to eight players. Teams line up, with one player facing the team. This player throws the ball to each team member in turn. The last person in each team to receive the ball runs round the back of the team to the front place, and takes the first pass of the new sequence. The game continues until everyone has had a turn.

• **Circular passing rounders:** the four teams form a square, with a thrower from each team in the middle. The last child in each team to receive the ball runs around the three other teams (ie around the square) to take the first place and restart the sequence (Fig 18b).

Team A

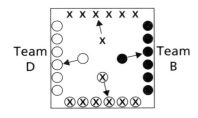

Team D

Team B

Team C

Fig 18b

Coach:
variety in passing to free (unmarked) players, eg over and underarm; running to space after pass to receive ball; keeping eyes on the ball; shielding ball by pivoting and screening with body; faking or feinting a pass to beat opponent; no body contact or running with the ball; one-to-one marking in defence; bounce and roll passes; sideways/back passes.

• **Bench ball:** 3v3, 4v4, 5v5, etc, using a large ball and two benches (either end of hall or court). Each team aims to pass the ball to their player standing on one of the benches; this player may move along the bench to catch a scoring pass from any direction. A scorer may replace the player on bench. Start, and restart after a score with a centre pass from the middle (see figure 19).

Fig 19: bench ball

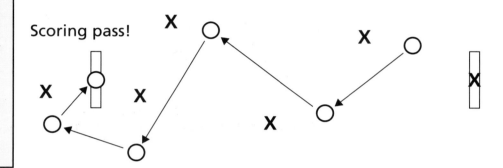

Scoring pass!

If outdoors, three or four games can be played across a netball court. If indoors, adapt to conditions. It may help to have no end lines or sidelines, therefore allowing rebounds, for a more continuous flow. It may be safer to restrict movement near the scoring area to avoid overcrowding (eg by drawing a 'no-go' area round the bench).

Coach:
Pivoting to screen the ball from opponent; looking for players in free spaces to pass to; only dribbling if space is available; feinting before passing; using lateral vision when passing; signalling (by hand) when in a free space; variety of passes.

• **Circle ball/mat ball:** played as bench ball, but teams pass to their player standing on a bench inside a large circle (eg 3 m diameter) or a large mat area (eg 8x4 m). Scoring passes can be made from any direction, in front or behind the bench or mat. Attackers and defenders not allowed in the circle.

• **Court ball:** played as bench ball but across one-third netball court width. Scoring is by passing to player on bench, or standing along end line. Gradually introduce netball rules .
Note: Adjustable posts can be used at this stage. Score one point if ring is hit, two points if ball enters net (adjust and lower height according to age or ability).

• **Mini basketball:** use scoring system as for bench ball or court ball but allow running and bouncing the ball. Once bouncing sequence has stopped, ball must be passed or the player must try a scoring shot.

Use a mixture of these games within a grid to give a wide experience of junior netball/basketball (see figure 9 and pp74-75).

Fig 20: Example of a small games grid

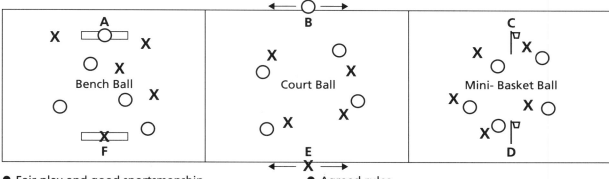

- Fair play and good sportsmanship.
- 1 player per team can arbitrate if disagreement.

- Agreed rules.
- Players rotate anti-clockwise every 4–5 mins to vary game and opponents. A→F→E→D→C→B→A

Football skills

With medium/large playballs (one each) or light playballs (Frido type) for practice:
- Find different ways to dribble, change direction and stop the ball with your feet.
- Roll the ball, one foot at a time, in different ways: a) close to you; b) all over play area.
- Walk/jog and dribble ball. Stop ball on signal or in own time (wedge ball with side of foot).
- Wedge the ball between knees, ankles or feet and jump in different directions.
- Practice jumping over the ball: a) while stationary; b) while on the move.
- Dribble in and out of cones, hoops, etc. Use instep/outside of foot for ball control.
- Find different body parts on which to: a) balance the ball; b) rebound the ball.
- Bounce the ball on different body parts to catch or bounce and trap with foot.
- Find different ways to stop ball bouncing, with feet/legs/chest/head (trapping, controlling).
- Throw (light) ball up a few centimetres to head in different ways.

In pairs
- Overhead throw (soccer throw-in) for partner to stop, control and pass back.
- Underarm lob for partner to head back (very close at first); six each (o).
- Keep the ball up by rebounding it off different parts of your body (one bounce allowed between each rebound); have two or three attempts, then change over. Score number of rebounds multiplied by number of body parts used.

Coach:
eyes on ball; using front of head (forehead); rocking into ball from legs through trunk, to head ball forward.

(o)

Footskills
Passing (in pairs)
- Use different parts of your foot to pass to a partner: instep, toe, outside, top, heel.
- In pairs, five to ten metres apart. Pass ball gently and stop with instep (non-kicking foot alongside ball) before returning the pass.

- Dribble ball to cone, pass to partner on return.
- Pass to partner through cones or beanbags, one or two metres apart. Invent a game using the cones.
- Pass along a marked line.
- Pass to partner; run to a new position five to six metres away and call for partner to pass to you. Keep changing direction. Stop ball and control with feet before passing again.
- Pass directly to each other without stopping the ball.
- Pass on the move, with two or three touches to control ball before passing (pass into space for partner to run on to the ball).
- Pass on the move avoiding cones/skittles spaced in a line.
- Face partner four to five metres apart. Dribble ball through partner's legs, round partner and back. Pass to partner (p).
- Long passes, partners 20 m apart: kick under ball, lean back to lift (chip) ball to partner.

(p)

Mild competition and challenge can be used when appropriate, eg how many passes in a set time?

Small-group and team activities using footskills

- 2v1, 3v1: one intercepts while others interpass, passing and running to new positions. How many successful passes in 60 seconds?
- Corner spry (football) using direct passes and stop and pass (four per team) (q).
- In pairs. One dribbles and shields ball with body, while partner tries to gain possession from front to side. No body contact!
- Small relays with three or four per team, well spaced in line behind each other. Each player: (i) dribbles to line and back; (ii) dribbles to line and passes back, then runs to back of team; (iii) dribbles around team, in and out of legs; (iii) stands opposite another, passes and runs after ball to back of opposite line (Fig 21 (i-iii)).
- With partner. Pass ball through small goals (marked with cones one to two metres apart) around edge of playing area. Allow four passes between each goal attempt. Emphasis on co-operative play and running off the ball to receive next pass. Ball can enter goals from either side.

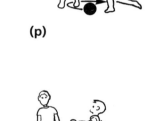

(q)

Invasion games using footskills

- One ball per child. Players dribble in confined area, approximately 20 x 20 m, shielding ball from three or four who tackle (no body contact) from the front. Change tacklers when possession gained, or on signal.
- As above but children can score through goals from either side, cones two or three metres apart, spaced around edge of playing area.

The size of pitch and number of tacklers can be increased to suit the ability of the children. As skill increases, small games of 2v1 or 3v1 can be introduced using the same model (Fig 21 (iv)).

Fig 21: Games to develop footskills

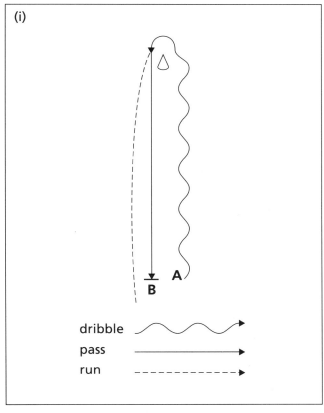

(i)

dribble

pass

run

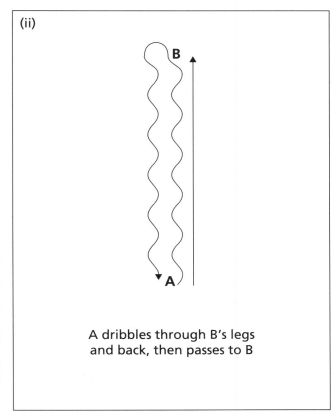

(ii)

A dribbles through B's legs
and back, then passes to B

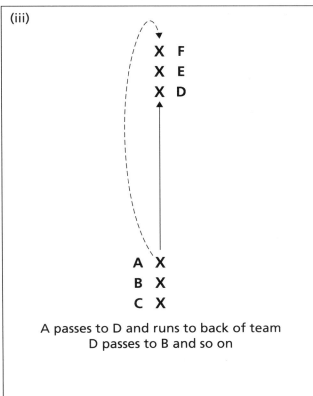

(iii)

A passes to D and runs to back of team
D passes to B and so on

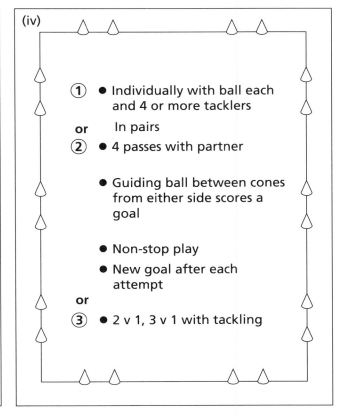

(iv)

① ● Individually with ball each
and 4 or more tacklers

or In pairs

② ● 4 passes with partner

● Guiding ball between cones
from either side scores a
goal

● Non-stop play

● New goal after each
attempt

or

③ ● 2 v 1, 3 v 1 with tackling

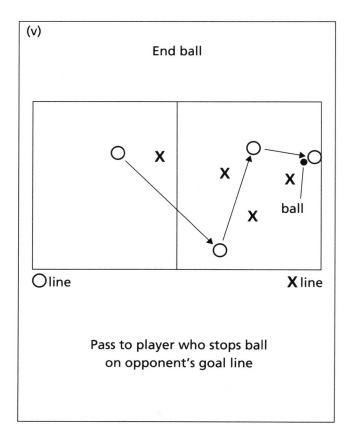

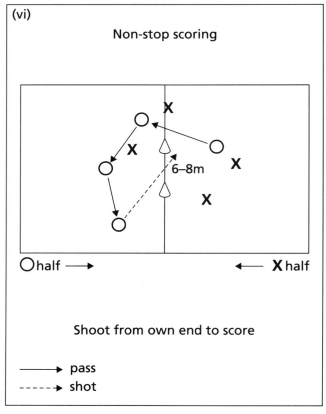

Fig 21

Coach:
one-on-one marking in defence; wall passes in attack; calling and signalling when in free space; need for rules and fair play; good sportsmanship; accepting decisions.

End ball
A game for 3v3 or 4x4 using an area 20 x 20 m, marked by cones and halfway line. The aim is to trap ball along the opponent's goal line by dribbling and passing, and score a goal anywhere along the line.

Development:
• With/without dribbling.
• Introduce throw-ins and heading.
• Introduce restricted areas of movement for individuals, eg left, right.
• Introduce signalling for direction of pass and calling for pass when in empty space.
• Introduce goal scored if headed over opponent's end line.
• Introduce small goals to shoot through from within a five-metre marked area: no goalkeepers.
• Devise a football game with one goal only: try several different ideas.
• Try non-stop scoring using one goal at centre and no goalkeeper.
• With goalkeeper. Try one, two, three or four touches of ball before passing to score from own end. Restart by rolling ball along centre line.
• Play with rush goalkeeper who also acts as defender.
• Positions: left, right, attack, defence (begin to restrict areas of movement to avoid crowding). Players to be in opponent's half for goal to count.
• Introduce other rules gradually: fair tackles from front and side; handball; obstruction; dangerous play; restart game from centre with bounce or free pass after a goal scored; headed goals score double.
• Introduce five- or six-a-side games (with or without goalkeepers) using half pitch/large grids 30 x 30 m.

Rugby skills

Resources: moulded plastic rugby (or round) balls sizes 3 and 4; small 'softy' balls are ideal for 7–8 year-olds.

Children will need time to get used to an oval-shaped ball before feeling confident about using it. Start by letting them pass it to and fro. Discuss the peculiarities of the ball. Questions to ask include:

- What are the different ways of holding the ball? Which is best?
- What does the ball do as it moves through the air?
- What is the best way to throw it? What is the best way to catch it?

See Ball skills (pp82,83) for skills development and games involving holding, carrying, passing, catching and running with the ball. Other rugby activities include:

- Free running in different directions holding a ball in two hands along its length (one ball for each child).
- As above. On signal, place (don't drop) ball firmly on the ground; continue running. At next signal, pick up another ball and continue stopping and dodging.
- Practise different ways to pick up your ball on the move. Discuss the best methods.
- Find different ways to toss your ball in the air and catch it.
- With a partner. Practise ways to pass and catch the ball, starting two to three metres apart; standing sideways on, both facing the same direction, pass backwards and forwards; progress to walking, jogging, then running.
- In pairs. Run towards marker; at halfway point put the ball down/fall down with ball behind you (don't release ball until you are on the ground, your back facing the imaginary opponents); on return, pick ball up and pass to partner, who repeats.
- As above, but partner runs three metres behind you and picks ball up; both continue running to marker, passing ball; then return to starting point.
- In grid approximately 10 x 10 m, passing and running in pairs (four pairs per grid) avoiding others, dodging, stopping, creating space.
- In threes, 2v1, piggy in middle, running and passing, feinting, changing direction (no passes above head height). Count caught passes in 60 seconds, or aim to achieve ten passes before changing chaser.
- As above, 3v1. Chaser aims to intercept pass, or touch carrier at waist level with both hands. Change roles. Count passes in timed session (60 seconds).
- Ball tag 3v1 or 4v1. Aim to touch free player, with ball, by running and passing in all directions. Change roles with tagger. Count how many touches in 60 seconds.

> **Coach:**
> approaching alongside the ball, bending knees, scooping up the ball with both hands.

> **Coach:**
> cradling ball into the body, making a basket with hands and arms, reaching and bringing the ball into your body.

> **Coach:**
> turning the shoulders; swinging arms back and through to follow path of ball; aiming in front of partner, tummy height. Gradually introduce no forward pass.

- In grid approximately 10 x 10 m, 3v3, rugby touch and pass. Aim to touch ball over opponent's line; two-handed touch means ball must be released or passed backwards. Game restarts with backward pass at centre.
- Practise 1v1, 2v2 scrums; no pushing; straight backs; heads up and under opponent's collar bone; hips low, knees flexed. Emphasise restarting the game by guiding (hooking) ball back into play with instep.

Development:
- Plan rules together, eg: How do you restart after a try? After ball is out of play?
- Hold ball in two hands, run forward into space.
- Support the ball carrier, to the side and slightly behind, to receive a pass.
- One-on-one marking.
- Introduce dropped ball (knock on) rule: restart with free pass, opponents five metres away.
- Introduce conditions (eg no overhead pass; three passes before try can be scored).
- Increase size of grid; try games of 4v2, 4v3, 4v4, 5v5.
- Restart by introducing 2v2 scrum after forward pass and knock on.
- In fours. Pass the ball across a large grid, along the diagonal line and back and score a try at the end. If ball is dropped, all stop, realign and restart with pick up and pass. How many passes before a try is scored?
- As above, but first player kicks the ball a few metres ahead, then picks up and passes to partner.

For further development of skills and training refer to *Mini Rugby – the Real Thing* and *New Image Rugby*, both published by the Rugby Football Union (RFU).

Striking/fielding skills for rounders, cricket and hockey

Resources: tennis balls are best; soft rubber balls are cheaper; foam balls are especially useful indoors.

One ball each for the following activities which are useful for developing skills needed in small-ball games such as rounders and cricket.

Bouncing and catching
- Balance ball on palm/back of hand at different levels; now try other hand.
- As above, while walking, jogging, moving sideways, sitting, lying, or kneeling.
- Bounce ball and catch in a variety of ways: stationary, walking, running.
- As above, using one/both hands; low bounces and high bounces.
- Pat bounce the ball with the palm of the left/right hand (a tennis ball is best).

Coach:
holding ball in fingers, bending arm slightly above shoulder; twisting the body slightly sideways on, and flinging the ball through body, shoulder, arm and wrist.

Coach:
when standing close, watch ball carefully, concentrating, hands spread ready for action in a half-squat position, knees slightly bent, feet slightly apart, ready to move. When stopping/fielding at a distance, make a barrier with hands and legs if ball is moving fast, or bend low and scoop up the ball in two hands, ready to throw immediately to wicket/base/ partner.

Coach:
one foot forward (opposite to arm); turning body slightly; ball in fingers; toss ball and follow through with hand and arm.

- A bounce with a catch or pat (push) vary as follows:
  - in and out of a hoop/circle making a sequence of bounces.
  - invent a sequence while sitting, kneeling crouching.
  - look away from the ball (to a partner/teacher who holds up fingers to count) add, multiply etc.
- Bounce and catch ball: a) one handed; b) increasing distance from three to ten metres.
- Bounce ball into a hoop, coiled ropes or playground markings, and catch.
- Overarm, bounce ball and throw for power and distance. Find best ways to achieve this. Discuss and demonstrate first, then coach overarm throwing skills (see coaching hints).

Rolling and fielding

- Roll ball to partner for accuracy: a) to hit feet; b) between two cones placed at mid-point.
- Roll to partner, who picks up and returns with roll/bounce/overarm throw.
- With a partner. Standing together, A rolls ball away for B to chase, pick up and roll or throw back.
- In threes. A with one foot on a base (hoop), rolls/throws ball to B who fields and rolls ball to C, fielding close to A, who returns to A with roll or throw. Distances should be adjusted according to experience and ability.
- Discuss and try effective ways to stop and field the ball: a) when standing close to thrower/striker; b) when fielding at a distance.

Bowling

Underarm (for cricket, rounders, softball and other striking games):
- Find ways to bowl accurately to your partner – arm must be straight on delivery.
- Bowl to bounce ball into a hoop/marker two metres from your partner. Vary the distance apart from your partner, starting from eight metres.
- Bowl ball straight into your partner's hands, to be caught with no bounce.
- Bowl at a wall target; partner fields rebound: a) with a bounce; b) without a bounce

Overarm (as in cricket):
- Try bouncing ball to your partner, keeping a straight arm.
- Stand sideways to partner, both arms outstretched, ball held in fingers of near hand. Rock back then forward on to front foot to release ball with a straight arm to bounce near your partner.
- As above, bowling from cone/wicket to cone/wicket. Start ten metres apart and increase gradually to 18 m, according to ability.

> **Coach:**
> front foot and shoulder pointing to partner/target (sideways on); same action as above, but curl front arm up and across chest; weight on back foot, looking over shoulder at target; as weight transfers from back to front foot, releasing ball with a downward flick of wrist, keeping eyes on target; stepping forward to follow flight of the ball.

Add interest and motivation by
- Working with partner to achieve maximum score in set time.
- Counting number of successful hits or catches.
- Encourage teacher/pupil coaching roles as children help each other.
- Encourage inventing their own games to include the skills practised.

Small-group games and activities with small balls

Relay competitions

In teams of three to five children:

- Roll ball between legs, backwards, to last person, who runs to the front to repeat.
- As above, but ball is rolled along a bench.
- As above, but ball travels under legs and overhead alternately.
- A standing one to two metres in front, facing team, passes to each in turn; each player then sits or crouches down till last player returns the ball. B then replaces A at the front, and sequence is repeated (r).

Shuttle passing

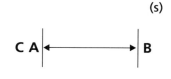

In teams of three:
A and C together, B ten metres away facing them. A passes to B and runs after the pass to take B's place; B passes to C, follows the pass and so on. Players stay behind lines to receive and send passes (s).

Corner spry

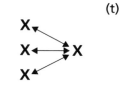

Passing in groups of three to five using rolling, bouncing, throwing techniques (t).

Shuttle relays

This game can be played in twos and threes, bouncing or throwing and catching on the run, round a cone and back to partner. The ball is handed, passed or placed on ground to execute changeover. The relays can be run as races, or executed in a set time to achieve a team score (u).

Cricket, rounders, softball skills

Resources: small cricket bat shape or flat rounders bat; tennis or airflow ball (according to area available):
- In pairs. Practice grip (pick up bat like an axe from the floor) and stance (stand sideways to bowler, eyes turned to face ball, bat ready raised or behind feet).

- A (bowler) underarms a ball with one bounce to B (striker) who hits back: a) straight; b) to left/right of bowler into the field.
- A underarms a ball with one bounce to B, to hit wall marking. B defends with bat.
- A underarms ball with no bounce (as in rounders) for B to hit back: a) low; b) for catch. B should stand in front of a wall to hit (saves time if ball is missed).
- Invent your own bat and ball game: a) in pairs; b) in fours (eg French cricket).

Development:
- Introduce scoring.
- Introduce a maximum number of hits/bowling sequence (children change roles).
- Introduce bowling underarm or overarm (if cricket).
- Introduce games with conditions, eg score a run only if ball is hit in front of wicket or base.

Circular cricket
A game for six players (see figure 22)

- All start with ten runs (or points).
- Six balls each, then all rotate positions.
- Score by: runs from the bat in front of the wicket; catching or bowling a player out (two points); batter loses two points if bowled, caught or run out.

Fig 22: Circular cricket

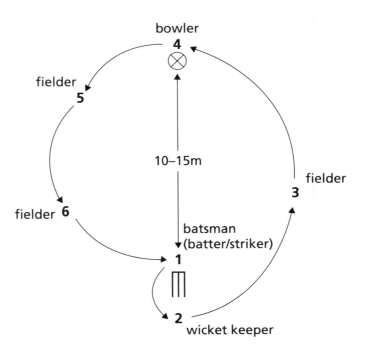

Circular rounders

A game for four or six players, using hoops as bases, flat rounders bats and tennis balls (see figure 23).

- Adjust pitch according to ability (two, three or four bases, 5 to 15 m apart).
- One player bowls (up to three bowls), one bats, the others field (behind and at bases).
- Balls bowled must be between knee and shoulder of batting child.
- Each batter is allowed three or more attempts, then all rotate one position.
- The batter is free to run to base one if last (third) batting attempt is missed.
- Score: one point if batter reaches first base, two points if second base is reached, etc; two points if fielder catches the ball when hit, before it bounces; two points if fielder throws to base and runs out batter.

These circular games can be continuous rotations, though normally two or three rotations will be sufficient.

Fig 23: Circular rounders

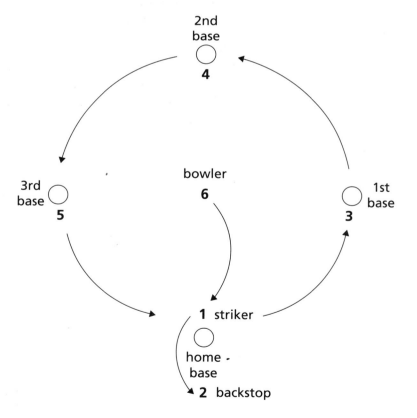

All rotate one position after striker has run
to gain furthest base

Non-stop cricket or rounders

A game for two teams of five or six a side. Runs are scored by running to and from a scoring base while the fielding team retrieves the ball and returns it to the bowler, who bowls whether the batter is back or not (see figure 24).

Fig 24: Non-stop cricket or rounders

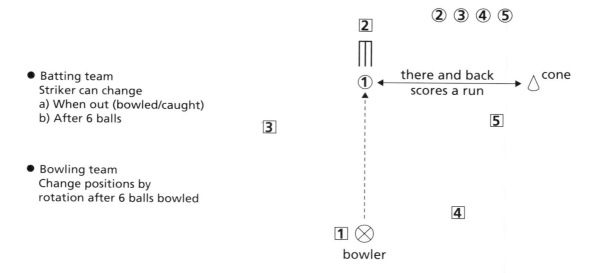

- Batting team
  Striker can change
  a) When out (bowled/caught)
  b) After 6 balls

- Bowling team
  Change positions by
  rotation after 6 balls bowled

Fig 25: Team rounders

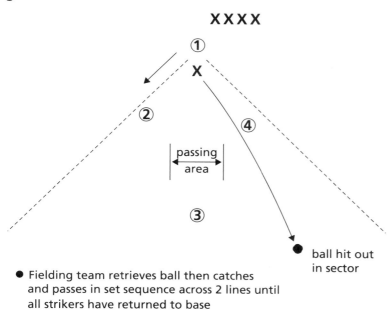

- Fielding team retrieves ball then catches
  and passes in set sequence across 2 lines until
  all strikers have returned to base

- Highest number of catches wins

- Teams can have 2 or 3 strikes and runs before changing over

Team rounders

The batting team takes turns to strike, kick, or throw a ball into the sector between base two and base four. The fielding team retrieves the ball: each member must give and catch a pass in sequence, while the entire batting team runs round all the bases (fielding team works out best method for each having a catch). The team scoring the highest number of passes wins (see figure 25).

A variation is for the batting team to perform a skill while running around bases (eg throwing, catching, bouncing or dribbling a ball each or in pairs).

Hockey skills

Examples of games include mini-hockey and shinty.
Resources: medium-size playballs, sponge balls, airflow balls and hockey sticks.

Show children how to hold a hockey stick: grip near the top of the stick with the left hand, making a 'V' between thumb and first finger (as if shaking hands with the stick), then curl fingers of right hand tightly around the stick to grip halfway down shaft (reverse if left-handed).

Controlling and dribbling

With a stick and a ball each:

> **Coach:**
> keeping bottom hand halfway down stick for close control; trying not to hit with back of blade; pushing ball out in front of feet; stopping by wrapping blade round the ball.

- Find different ways to walk, then jog, keeping ball close to stick face.
- Guide ball by keeping stick in contact with floor.
- Guide ball by pushing and patting with the stick.
- Dribble ball in different directions/around hoops/cones. Stop on signal. Use some of the footskills practices and activities with the above techniques (pp87-88).

Pushing and hitting

- In pairs. Push ball to partner, four to five metres away, keeping stick on the ground; push through the ball.
- Push ball to partner, who stops it and pushes it back.
- Walking and jogging, practise passing/pushing to partner, who collects ball, pushes, and dribbles a short distance before returning with a push-pass.
- Hitting gently (stick low to ground, be strict (50 cm is high enough)) to partner, who stops first before hitting back – increase distance to 15–20 m apart.

> **Coach:**
> when stopping, keeping bottom hand low on stick; keeping feet out of line.

Once these skills are learned, introduce practice games for footskills (pp88-89). No screening of the ball should be allowed, and be very strict about 'sticks' rule. (No sticks above shoulder height. It is safer to restrict to knee or waist height to begin.)

Net/wall games skills for volleyball and tennis

Volleyball
Resources: (volleyball) large light plastic (sizes 3 or 4) balls.

- Ask children to hold a large ball above their heads, spreading their hands wide so that they are looking at the backs of their hands.
- Holding ball as above, throw the ball in the air and catch it.
- As above, but ask children to make consecutive volleys in the air.

Note: children should bend their legs and straighten their arms as they push the ball into the air, flexing the wrists back and pushing up with fingers.

• Children to volley a ball into the air, let it bounce and (bending knees) try to volley it into the air again.
• Try volleying the ball in the air while walking round the area.
• Volley ball as high in the air as you can: how many times can you clap before it bounces?
• Volley ball into the air and try to turn round on the spot before it bounces.
• Practise these sending and receiving activities with a partner. Ask pairs to develop a sequence showing as many different volleying activities as possible.

Tennis

Resources: (tennis) small, light, short-handled wooden bats of various shapes, and airflow, sponge/tennis balls as appropriate. Allow for slightly larger balls where necessary.

One ball each:

• Find different ways to balance the ball on both sides of the bat.
• As above, while sitting/kneeling/crouching/standing.
• As above, while walking/jogging/avoiding obstacles/each other.
• Hit the ball gently up to bounce on the ground and hit again.
• Hit the ball down to bounce and hit again (pat bouncing).
• Hit the ball up in the air continuously – count how many times.
• Hit the ball up in the air while moving in different directions.
• Bat the ball against a wall to bounce, and hit again. Try this alone, then with a partner.
• Practise these with both hands, and backhand (turning wrist).

One ball between two:

• Hit ball from hand with bat for partner to catch: a) with bounce; b) without bounce.
• A bounces ball to B (striker) who hits back to A to catch.
• In pairs or fours. Hit the ball gently to each other with one or more bounces.
• Hit the ball gently to each other over a rope or line, with one bounce.
• Wall ball: rebound hitting alternately with one or more bounces.
• Hit airflow or shuttlecock up continuously: a) individually; b) with a partner.
• In pairs. As above, over a low net/rope.
• All these exercises should be practised forehand and backhand, or both hands.

Coach:
watching ball on to bat; moving feet quickly and early; turning sideways to play backhand; practising keeping bat face vertical; bending knees and hips to get down to hit; following through with the shot; encouraging co-operative practice for highest consecutive number of hits.

Short tennis games

Use small courts 8 x 4 m or 10 x 5 m, with cones and canes or low benches as nets. Older children (years 5 and 6) can be encouraged to invent their own rules for scoring, serving, points, etc. Variations might include:

- Scoring up to 12 points.
- Maximum number of serves before change over (eg three or five).
- Scoring after every rally.
- Hitting randomly or alternately (as in table tennis).

Note: shuttlecocks can be used for all the above games, with a higher rope or net (as in badminton).

For more on Resources for Games see page 186.
For Assessment see pp169, 172.

Athletics

'Athletic activities concern the pursuit of the fulfilment of individual potential. Pupils strive to improve performance against measurements and/or others in maximising their performance in terms of time, height, length or distance. Athletic activities build on children's natural capacities to run, jump and throw. They promote all-round physical development – speed, strength, stamina and flexibility.'

(PE for ages 5–16, 1991)

Athletics has always been part of the curriculum in junior schools. Some schools have introduced specialist athletic programmes for their children, others have relied on lessons linked to a special event like sports day. The question of the advisability of competition has been an ongoing debate, and reflects a classic dilemma of teaching – how do you stretch the abilities of high achievers whilst being sensitive to the needs of the less able?

An athletics programme should support high achievers and provide the basis for all children to benefit from a health-related programme encouraging fitness for life. How is this to be achieved? One way is to follow a commercially produced award scheme (see Resources for information on these). Another is to create an athletics programme which clearly focuses on effort and improvement – and active involvement in athletics – rather than simply on levels of attainment. Athletics concerns the fulfilment of human potential; a progressive teaching programme appropriate to the age and development of children across the whole range of ability is needed. Athletics provides the framework for such a programme, and is divided into the following sections:
- What to teach
- Lesson planning
- Warm-up activities
- Running
- Skipping
- Jumping
- Throwing
- Assessment
- Sports days.

What to teach

athletics in the National Curriculum

The Statements of Attainment for PE in the National Curriculum say that at the end of Key Stage 2 pupils should be able to:

- plan, practise, improve, and remember more complex sequences of movement;
- perform effectively in activities requiring quick decision-making;
- respond safely, alone and with others, to challenging tasks, taking account of levels of skill and understanding;
- swim unaided for at least 25 m and demonstrate understanding of water safety;
- evaluate how well they and others perform and behave against criteria suggested by the teacher and suggest ways of improving performance;
- sustain energetic activity over appropriate periods of time in a range of physical activities and understand the effects of exercise on the body.

The Programme of Study for Athletics says that pupils should:

- Practise and develop basic activities of running (over shorter and longer distances, and in relays), throwing and jumping.
- Be given opportunities for guidance in measuring, comparing and improving their own performance.
- Experience competitions, including those they make up for themselves.

Units of work that aim to cover the Statements of Attainment and Programmes of Study should include:

Running activities	Jumping activities	Throwing activities
• Sprinting, jogging	• Free jumping	• Overarm throwing
• Starting, stopping	• Long and high jump	• Bounce throws
• Free running	• Hurdling	• Rebound throws
• Team and relay runs	• Skipping	• Target throws
• Timed races	• Team jumping	• Field and team

These activities should feature throughout the junior stage and children will respond at different levels, so the emphasis should be on personal performance, improvement and enjoyment. Teachers should adapt or simplify athletic tasks to meet the needs of their children.

Athletic activities in this book are graded in difficulty so that the early activities will be specially useful for introducing a new skill to children in years 3 and 4. Most activities are suitable for class, group or individual teaching, and lesson planning should take account of different ways of grouping children for athletics.

Lesson planning

The following are some points to remember when preparing for PE:

Before the lesson
- Children should change into PE kit, eg PE vest in team/school colours, shorts, trainers, and warm clothing, such as a track suit.
- Are you changed into trainers, sweatshirt or track suit?
- Be positive about cold weather – all the more reason to be active!
- Carry a memo card listing planned activities.
- Check equipment beforehand: ensure it is ready and well dispersed for ease of access.
- Changing, and walking to and from the activity are part of the lesson. Expect control, quiet, and consideration for others. Be strict – it sets the tone for the lesson.
- Be prepared for a wet weather alternative – is the hall available? Can you switch the lesson time? Can you teach another PE activity, eg dance, gymnastic or indoor athletic activities?

During the lesson
Make sure that everyone is active for as much of the lesson as possible!

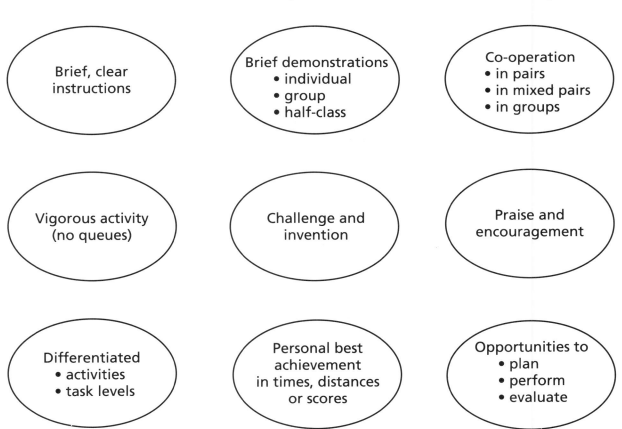

Brief, clear instructions

Brief demonstrations
- individual
- group
- half-class

Co-operation
- in pairs
- in mixed pairs
- in groups

Vigorous activity (no queues)

Challenge and invention

Praise and encouragement

Differentiated
- activities
- task levels

Personal best achievement in times, distances or scores

Opportunities to
- plan
- perform
- evaluate

Lesson plans

Athletic activities may take place with games activities as part of an outdoor PE lesson, or be performed in isolation as an athletics lesson. The following are the suggested elements of a PE lesson which focuses on athletics:

- **Warm up** (3–4 mins): Energetic, heart-related activity, eg jogging, jumping, hopping, and stretching activities (especially arms, shoulders, trunk and legs).
- **Skills development** (10 mins): involving either: whole-class skills practised by individuals and pairs, or varied athletic activities in groups; or varied games/athletic activities.
- **Group activities** (10–15 mins): involving either: small-group activities, eg working co-operatively to achieve maximum scores; group competition, eg six of similar ability in a group, working with a partner, adding activity scores together, competing against other pairs; personal achievement challenges, eg working in groups, keeping personal records of achievement; whole-class activities, eg relay races, jogging events or longer races for personal achievement.
- **Ending** cool-down activities (3–4 mins): controlled stretching and strengthening activities; evaluation and target-setting for the next athletics lesson.

Warm-up activities

Athletics lessons generally have a similar format to all other PE lessons, but even more care should be taken with the important warm-up period, which is vital before beginning any athletic activity. Juniors are especially enthusiastic and competitive at athletics; they can easily extend their efforts beyond their capabilities, risking muscle strain or ligament damage. The following warm-up activities enable each joint of the body to be exercised, and will increase heart and respiratory rates. A sample warm-up schedule is also given. You will need to vary your warm-up schedules according to the weather, and the number of repetitions each activity requires. Choose from the following:

Warm ups

- **On the spot:** stretching movements (see Stretching activities pp77, 105), jogging, stride jumps, squat jumps.

- **Walking:** walk around the area slowly then quickly, speeding up then slowing down, walking quickly and stopping on command.
- **Striding:** walk with long strides, slowly (over 'stepping stones'), then quickly ('giant steps').
- **Jogging:** jog on the spot for one minute, jog around area slowly, quickly, slowly: stop.
- **Side-stepping:** side-step to the right, then left, fast and slow, dodging others.
- **Running:** run around area, dodging others, forwards and backwards; on signal, touch ground with one or both hands, run, and stop on command.
- **High-stepping:** jog or run on the spot, lifting knees high. On signal, jog around area lifting knees high.
- **Hopping:** hop on the spot, then around the area; right leg then left leg.
- **Skipping:** skip round the area, alternate hopping, skipping and striding.
- **Jumping:** jump in the air using both feet; jump (feet together) or leap around the area.
- **Balancing:** choose one line (real or imaginary); balance along it, walking/jumping, walking forwards and backwards.
- **Patterns:** walk/jog/run to make different shapes and patterns, eg spell your name in big letters over the area.
- **Sequences:** on given signal or free choice perform two or more activities in sequence, eg hop/skip/jump, run/stop/squat jump, run/star jump.
- **Destinations:** run all over the area touching as many walls/lines/children as you can.
- **Moving in pairs:** follow partner's shadow, copy movements on the spot/all over area (changing leaders often).
- **Class tag games:** free tag, pair tag, chain tag, release tag (Stuck in the mud).
- **Class warm-up games:** children run to side/area on given signals,eg Traffic lights, Pirates, Shipwreck, Longboat, etc (see Games pp78-79).

Stretching activities
- **Reaching:** stretch/reach as high, wide or long as possible.
- **Curling:** curl as small as possible; alternate stretching and curling.
- **Arms:** swinging, circling, pressing forwards/backwards/sideways, using one then both arms; practise throwing actions.
- **Wrists and fingers:** rotate wrists; move them backwards/forwards, shake them, spread fingers wide, clench fists; make wrists and fingers dance in the air!
- **Shoulders:** lifting up and down, rotating, pressing back with arms sideways, hands joined above head.
- **Trunk:** bending from the waist, twisting right and left, arching backwards.

(a)

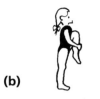

(b)

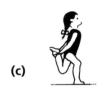

(c)

- **Neck:** rotate head gently; turn head left and right; lower chin on to chest; move head back. Hold each position for three to four seconds.
- **Reach back:** try to grasp hands together behind back (left then right hand over left/right shoulder).
- **Lean forward:** lean forward to take weight on front foot, to stretch hamstring muscles of back leg (a).
- **Knees:** Clasp each knee in turn to your chest (b).
- **Hamstrings:** pull and lift heel to touch bottom (c).
- **Ankles:** circle ankles first to right then left; up then down; shake each foot.
- **Jump stretch:** from standing position, make a star jump/stretch jump/ tucked jump.
- **Touching toes**: bending forwards with straight legs, touch ankles, toes, then floor; touch feet with opposite hands.
- **Sit and stretch:** sit down, stretch legs in front, touch ankles and toes; flex feet, point toes forwards and backwards; stretch legs wide; touch toes.
- **Press-ups:** show how to do press-ups (see p78) on hands and knees (d).

(d)

- **Squat thrusts:** crouch down, jump, pushing both legs back, jump, legs back to hands, in crouched position again.
- **Stretch shapes:** stretch into letter shapes, eg X, by stretching arms and legs wide.
- **Sequences:** children to perform given or own sequence of two or more stretches.
- **Paired stretching:** children to practise right- and left-hand pulls with partner, to support partner in arching trunk backwards, when attempting stretch paired shapes (e and f).

(e)

(f)

Class organisation

Athletics lessons can be organised in a variety of ways after the warm up, for example:

- **Whole-class lessons** with a single focus, ensuring sufficient apparatus for individual, pair and small-group work. This is especially useful when introducing new skills for Year 3 children, or when control needs to be exercised firmly.
- **Half the class** focuses on the same activity, half the class on small-group activity.
- **One group** focuses on new activity, with other groups on known activities.

Most activities for juniors will be centred round the three core areas of running, jumping and throwing as described in the following sections.

Running

'Now here, you see, it takes all the running you can do, to stay in the same place. If you want to get somewhere else, you must run at least twice as fast as that!' *(Lewis Carrol (Alice in Wonderland))*

Training to develop skill, strength and stamina in one or more of the key areas of athletics should be the main focus for each lesson. Children should be shown the techniques to improve each athletic skill; they should experience a variety of activities in which to practise the skills, and to develop the strength and stamina that will improve their performance. Running has, since the time of the Greeks (eg, as in the story of the runner from the battle of Marathon), been the central activity of athletics. The following activities will help to develop skills, strength and stamina in running.

Sprinting

Children should be encouraged to practise the correct sprinting technique. When they run they should lean forward and bend and swing their arms. Encourage them as they run, to drive their arms forward and lift their knees, taking long strides, and looking straight ahead. They should focus on forward movements, with no lateral or sideways deviation. They should run on the balls of their feet rather than flat-footed. Give them time to practise this, and show them ways of training to improve their performance, for example:

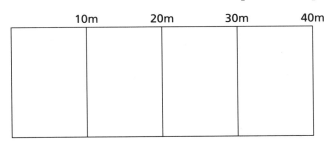

Track marked every 10m for sprinting activities

- Running gently, keeping upright, feeling light and springy on your toes.
- Running across area, lifting knees up to hip height, then taking longer strides.
- Sprint to first marker/cone/line, jog slowly to second, then sprint to the third (15 to 30 m apart).
- Hop on one leg across the area, then back on the other.
- Run on the spot, then run across area, synchronising arm and leg movements.
- Increase speed: walk, jog then run gradually faster in a straight line to 30 m or 40 m marker; slowly jog back.
- Different running speeds; eg practise quarter speed, half speed and full speed.
- Sprint with partner (alternately) to line, or around cone and back; touch hands to go.
- Shuttle relay: in threes or fours, run 30–40 m, pass beanbag to next in line.
- Baton relay: in teams of four, around 25 m cone and back.

• Team sprinting: teams of four jog in line around area. On signal (or when ready), back child sprints to front of team. Continue until each child has sprinted.
• Own relays: in fours. Children invent their own sprint relay races (maximum 80 m distance).
• Individual races over 50 or 80 m distances, in ability groups, for personal best times.

Starting and sprinting

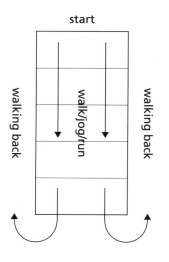

Getting off to a good start is a skill that needs practising. For juniors, a half-crouch start is best: arms akimbo, feet apart and ready to drive forward; hips and knees bent, looking five metres ahead, listening, waiting for 'Go!' signal. It can help for a child to imagine a coiled spring, or bullet ready to be fired from a gun. Here are some activities that can help children:
• Practise fast starts on command, eg 'On your marks, get set, go!' or use whistle signal.
• Try different starting positions; which is best for you?
• Timed sprints. Teacher times with stopwatch; each child tries to improve their personal best times over 20, 30, 40 m.
• In pairs. One coach, one athlete, to encourage/help/advise each other, eg using one or two points or reminders from a checklist before each sprint.

Team relays

Relays can have the benefits of both co-operative and competitive activity. They can help children to work with others, and strive to improve performance. As with all athletic skills, relay running improves with guidance and practice. The following activities can help develop relay-running skills:

Baton passing and shuttle relays

• Children in groups of three or four. Discuss and experiment to find the best, safest and quickest way to pass the baton or beanbag in preparation for relay.

• Try different ways of passing the baton; for example: baton held up in front at chest height (best for shuttle relay head-on exchange) and received in two hands for extra safety (g) or baton held to side at hip height (h). Practise baton-passing techniques first when walking, then jogging, then sprinting.

(g)

(h)

or

(i)

Shuttle or circular relays

Shuttle runs can be made by running round a cone before the baton change. A running change (i) can be used here. Children can find their own best way before the teacher coaches the following points:

- try to run off at the speed of the incoming runner;
- look behind you, turning slightly sideways;
- arm out, palm of hand upwards, to receive baton into the palm of the hand.

Team races

- Run team relay races for personal best times for the team, eg 4 x 50 m, 4 x 80 m, etc.
- Team of four race over 300 – 400 m; children decide which distance each team member will cover (minimum 50 m). Vary distances according to age and ability.

Running longer distances

Longer distance running is good for building up stamina – remind children about the legend of the runner from the battle of Marathon! Discuss local fun runs and runners; then try these longer distance running activities:

- **Training runs:** practise relaxed running at quarter, half and three-quarter speed over 100 m, 150 m or 200 m.
- **Fun run:** jog around a field or local park, negotiating occasional obstacles (over, round or through).
  Have fun: go round trees, up hills; offer occasional challenges, eg 'See if you can find ...' (include cross-curricular observations and activities (see p161)).
- **Jogging trail:** create a jogging or walking trail around the school grounds, utilising a variety of both existing obstacles and created obstacles (eg cones). Ask children to help in designing this. Map the jogging trail so that all know the route to take.
- **Longer runs:** adjust distance to suit age, from 400 –1,000 m, for personal best times. Children can have a staggered start, in groups of similar ability (eg starting every ten seconds).
- **Interval runs:** walk/jog in single file of up to six. Child from back runs to front and all repeat around circuit.

It is essential that children should not be asked to run 800+ metres until they have walked and jogged the distance. This should be achieved gradually, over several weeks, for example:

- Week 1: walk briskly for 400 m.
- Week 2: jog gently, or jog and walk for 400 m.
- Week 3: jog gently, or jog and walk for 800 m.
- Week 4: children can try jogging for 800 m.

Skipping activities

The following activities link running and jumping through the development of skipping skills. Each child should have their own skipping rope, and find a space in which to practise. Allow children to try different rope lengths to find one that suits best. They should be allowed opportunities to observe each other as well as to practise on their own. A skipping demonstration by the teacher will always arouse interest!

Learning to skip
• Ask children to skip in any way they can: on the spot or on the move if they are able.
• Revise/teach skipping techniques – start with rope behind the ankles, arms bent fairly wide, wrists flexible; swing rope forward over head to the floor, step over rope, stop still and repeat.
• How many times can you step over/walk over/jump over the rope?
• Swing the rope faster; count the number of consecutive times you can step/walk/jump over the rope without stopping.
• Try a double-foot jump over rope, using same progression as above.
• Add a small bounce jump in between big jumps/skips.

Developing skipping skills
Once children can skip, encourage them to:

• Create different ways to skip on the spot, and on the move.
• Try skipping with rope swinging backwards.
• Skip forwards/backwards adding a sideways swing of the rope between skips.
• Skip and turn on the spot.
• Skip forwards while running/jumping/hopping.
• Develop their own sequence of different skipping movements.

Skipping with a partner
• Match your partner's skipping movements on the spot and on the move.
• In pairs. Skip together with one rope, side by side.
• In pairs. Skip together with one rope, facing each other.
• In pairs. Skip together with one moving in and out of the rope-jumps.
• Devise a sequence of skipping activities with a partner.
• In threes or fours, with a long rope: one or two skip, while two turn the rope.

Other skipping activities include synchronised skipping to a rhythm in pairs, groups or the whole class; and skipping to music.
Safety: Beware of skipping races, which can cause accidents unless the track has wide lanes and a safe grassed surface on which to run, and skippers are very competent.

Jumping

'Getting over that was the happiest moment of my life' *(10 year-old high jumper)*

Jumping involves developing strength of spring and a skilful landing. There are five basic jumps that need practising – jumping from two feet to two feet (the broad jump); two feet to one foot; one foot to the other foot; one foot to two feet; and one foot to the same foot. Children should be shown the best techniques for different kinds of jump, including the broad jump, long jump, high jump and hop-step-and-jump.Children should have the chance to practise jumping on their own, and then be given opportunities to improve their performance. The following activities will help develop skill and success in jumping:

Jumping activities

Try different ways of jumping; can children discover the five basic jumps?

(j)

- **Run and jump:** take two or three spring steps to jump as high or as far as you can.
- **Standing broad jump** using floor marking: toes on line, feet together; jump as far as you can, landing on two feet. Partner measures distance jumped by counting number of footsteps from where heel landed to start-line. Try again to better this distance (j).• **Jump back:** as above, but try to jump back over take-off line from landing mark.
- **Jump challenge:** lay two markers, eg ropes/beanbags, on floor; can child jump from one to the other? Increase/reduce distance to find maximum jump.
- **High jumps:** take two or three spring strides and jump high over imagined bar or rope (kick up legs as in 'scissors-style' high jump).
- **Hop jumps:** take two or three spring strides to hop as high as possible; swing up arms and non-take-off leg.
- **Obstacle jumps:** practise jumping over low obstacles, eg skittles, ropes, canes, partner curled up on floor!
- **Turning jumps:** practise jumping high and turning in the air before landing.
- **Successive jumps:** in teams. Each child takes turns to jump (feet together) in and out of four hoops laid on the ground about 30 cm apart; as individuals: see how many hoops they can jump into in 20 or 30 seconds (k).

(k)

hoops 30 cm. apart
adjust accordingly

Long jump

The essence of success in long jumping is to run fast and jump for lift, reach for a long landing. The arms, hips and knees should all help in the lift; feet should be forward on landing. Take-off should be with toe as close to the take-off line as possible. Landing should be forwards, not falling or stepping backwards. Coach these points one at a time. The following are some activities to help develop long-jump skills:

(l)

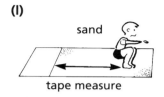

tape measure

ensure firm heel mark at take off point

- **Standing long jump:** two-foot take-off and landing; partner measures distance from landing heel mark to take-off.
- **Short-run long jump:** allow a four- to five-pace run-up; practise landing in sand or on mat.
- **Long-run long jump:** as above, increasing run-up to ten paces; land in sand or on double mat thickness (l).

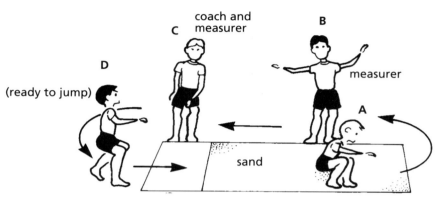

Fig 26: team jumping

Rotate roles: A — B — C — D — A (etc)

- **High and long jump:** practise jumping over low rope or cane (30–40 cm high) to gain height in jump before landing.
- **Team jumping:** in teams of four; one measuring, one marking (heel mark), one jumping, one preparing to jump. Team rotates duties. Measure from heel mark in sand (or on mat) to the take-off point. Distances scored by each child can be added together to make a team score (Figure 26).
- **Group jumping:** four children jump at once, across and into a jumping pit, coach standing at side to teach and encourage best efforts (m).

Children can jump from a wide take-off area, so that 'no jumps' are not a factor. Measurement (if appropriate) can be made from toe-mark (close observation required!)

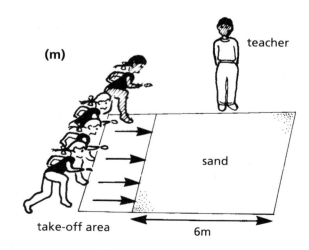

(m)

teacher

sand

take-off area   6m

High jump

There is no one best method of high jumping. Encourage children to experiment with and to take note of different methods, including:

• scissors style (most popular): kicking both legs high, one after the other;
• hopping and twisting;
• rolling and turning;
• hurdling (this should be discouraged as it is only effective at low heights).

The scissors style is generally the most popular and successful style for juniors. Note which take-off foot the child uses, and coach them to take off from the opposite side, ie left-foot take-offs will begin on the right of the bar. Coach making the lift as vertical as possible; having a springy run; swinging up with arms and swinging leg. Focus on one of these points at a time. Practise some skills separately, eg bouncy running, swinging and lifting each leg, swinging arms, and vertical jumping. Encourage children to look at the style of other children who are good models. If you are confident, be a good high jump model yourself!

Safety note: if children jump above one metre some may begin to land on their backs, in imitation of the 'Fosbury' style used by most athletes. In those cases, a proper regulation landing mattress must be used. Try to encourage a vertical jump, and landing on the feet if possible. More advanced techniques are best left to an athletics jumping coach at a club where correct training and proper facilities are available.

The following activities will help children develop their high jump skills:

• **Low jumps:** in groups of three. Two children hold a rope at low height to ensure jumping success, the third practises jumping from left, right and in front. Change roles every two to three jumps. If jumps are over 70 cm high, and on a hard surface, land on a gym mat.
• **High jump practice:** in similar-ability groups of five or six, with teacher present. One set of high jump equipment, double gym mats or sandpit and a weighted rope or lightweight flexible or collapsible bar are required. Children try jumping for success in any style they choose, and from different angles, to find which one suits them best. Ensure low heights for all to succeed.
• **High jump training:** as above, but encourage experimenting with methods of jumping high, with coaching and practise to improve performance.
• **Team jumping:** groups of four to six children encourage each other to reach their maximum height. Group shares duties, eg two to replace bar, one to judge, one to jump, one waiting to jump. If child fails to clear bar two or three times jumping stops. If appropriate, team adds their best individual heights together, or children compete against each other.

Coach:
running over canes (avoid jumping high); keeping low, leaning forward into running action; using the same lead leg; practising a regular number of steps between hurdles, eg five strides; encouraging rhythm and smooth action (older juniors can try a three-stride pattern between hurdles). Personal best times over three flights of hurdles, within a 50 m distance, can be encouraged.

Hurdling activities

Introductory activities for hurdling could include running over low obstacles, about 30 cm high. Use suitable obstacles to hurdle over, eg large balls, or canes on skittles. For older children the hurdle height can be raised to 40 cm. Allow the children to explore their own best ways to jump or run over canes before coaching them.

Safety points: always hurdle in one direction (never in reverse); never practise hurdling on wet grass or asphalt.

Organisation

Hurdling can be organised as a class activity, with four rows of six, seven or eight children running over two or three obstacles spread over 30–50m. On signal, children run in waves, then walk back to the start.

Hop, step and jump *(triple jump)*

Children should already have practised hopping, stepping and jumping in athletics, dance or gymnastics lessons. Hop, step and jump is simply these movements in a sequence. The following activities will help them to improve their performance:

- **Hopping:** ask children to hop on the spot, then across an area, changing legs on signal.
- **Stepping:** children practise leaping as far as they can, from one foot to the other.
- **Jumping:** children take a step then jump from one foot to land on two feet.
- **Hop/step/jump:** start with both feet together, hop onto one foot, and then step to the other and finally jump on two feet.
- **Hopscotch:** encourage children to play hopscotch on marked court to increase awareness of hop/step/jump techniques.

Note: in field athletics the hop/step/jump is called the triple jump; ask children to create and experiment with their own triple jump sequences from standing or a short run.

Throwing

'It never goes as far as you want it to ...'
(eight year-old)

Throwing overarm is one of the most difficult skills to acquire. It involves a complicated series of actions which must be properly co-ordinated to be successful. The most difficult aspect is to achieve the movement that transfers your body weight to the throw: following through with the body as the arm releases the thrown object, thus producing a long throw. Many children may still be finding the overarm throw difficult at the junior stage. Help them develop this skill by practising throwing from a straddled position: face the target and bend the throwing arm, keeping the forearm vertical; turn the body at the waist and move the throwing arm back so that the opposite shoulder faces the target; straighten, and thrust the throwing arm forward to release the ball. Try this technique from a kneeling position, then from a standing position.

The following activities will help children to improve their throwing technique and performance in throwing for distance:

- **Arm strengthening:** offer exercises to strengthen children's throwing arms, eg bunny jumps, press-ups and arm wrestling.
- **Large balls:** children to throw large balls overarm to their partners, using both hands: sitting, kneeling and standing; across various distances (n).

(n)

- **Chest throws:** using a large ball, children thow to their partner from their chests: sitting, kneeling and standing; try with tennis-sized ball.
- **Straddle throws:** sitting straddle-legged, facing partner, throw foam or tennis ball to partner over various distances; progress to bouncing ball to partner over five to six metres.
- **Kneeling throws:** as above, but kneeling on one knee (same knee as throwing arm), front arm bent across chest; as body turns, arm lifts back ready to throw. On release, front arm can swing naturally (o).
- **Standing throws:** as above, in standing position; bounce ball vigorously to partner, increasing distance to eight to ten metres (p).

(o)

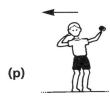

(p)

- **High bounces:** as above, but bouncing ball as high as possible: stand slightly sideways on, arm across chest, throwing arm right back; bend arm at elbow before explosive release.
- **Wall bounces:** throw ball against wall for partner to catch directly, or after one bounce; gradually increase distance from wall.
- **Target practice:** as above, but using wall target, eg marked concentric circles.
- **Distance throws:** in pairs 15–20 m apart. Throw to catch direct or after one bounce.

When a good overarm throwing action has developed, introduce a short three- or four-pace approach, with a sideways turn before release. Let children do this naturally, rather than teach specific steps. Now encourage a 45° angle of throw.

If throwing is taught as a class activity, children can work in pairs of similar ability; space them opposite a partner, along throwing lines which are 15–25 m apart. Nobody is to advance beyond the throwing line, and children throw only on teacher's signal (q).

Coach
(one point at a time): standing slightly sideways on, non-throwing arm across chest; leaning back, throwing arm straight; weight on rear leg, slightly bent; throwing by bending the elbow and flinging the ball up and forward; weight moving forward as ball is released at 30–45° angle.

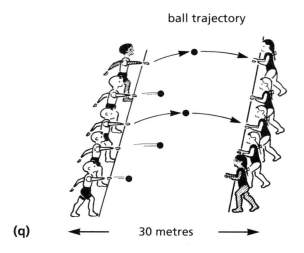

ball trajectory

(q) ←——— 30 metres ———→

Throwing can also be practised in team groups, as in the following illustration. Cones or markers are placed at five-metre intervals (measured in paces):

• groups of six children work as three pairs;
• children throw for personal best distance, measured by the markers;
• they keep behind the throwing line after the ball is thrown;
• pairs rotate after three throws, as throwers, distance markers, or ball retrievers;
• pairs of children may add their distances together (r).

(r)

• 3 balls available
• rotate anti-clockwise
• retriever retains ball ready to throw
• add scores in pairs or achieve a group aggregate

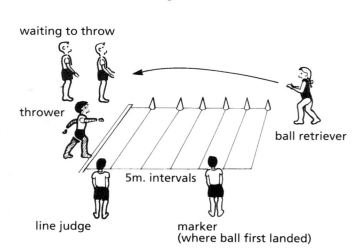

waiting to throw

thrower

ball retriever

line judge   5m. intervals

marker
(where ball first landed)

Under the direction of a PE teacher/coach indoor and outdoor practice is possible with foam or lightweight shot, discus and javelin (made by Eveque Leisure (see Resources (p189)), and may be useful for early experience of standing throws and correct throwing techniques; however, for most children, ball-throwing activities will be more suitable. Rounders and cricket balls can be used when children are mastering skills towards the end of Key Stage 2, but it is essential that children observe the safety rules, which should include the following:

Safety rules

- All behind the throwing line until everyone has thrown.
- Nobody to throw until the teacher's signal.
- Retrieve or catch balls only when the teacher says it is safe to do so.
- Throwing area should be clearly marked, eg by cones, and roped off if within a crowded field area.

Sports days

Sports days can be great fun if they are well organised, and provide opportunities for all to succeed at their level. They can also help meet many of the aims of the National Curriculum through activities involving planning, preparation and performing, for example:

- **Physical Education:** games and athletic skills practised through individual, pair and team activities, and health-related exercise;
- **English:** discussion, reading/writing letters, invitations, advertisements, programmes and reports;
- **Maths:** measuring, time and distance, and data handling;
- **Science:** links to 'My body' topics;
- **Geography:** maps/plans of sports area – Olympic Games topic.
- **Art and design:** posters, programmes and art theme: Sports Day;
- **Personal/social education:** co-operation, competition, leadership and responsibility.

How can we plan sports days to meet these cross-curricular aims, and answer the concerns and doubts about the educational value of the event? Can we provide opportunities for all to succeed at their own level? Can we ensure that all participate and are kept as active as possible? Can we organise sports within the constraints of school timetables and sustain the interest of the children? The following models are examples of the ways sports days may be organised. Few schools will adopt such a rigid approach as the traditional model, preferring to adapt a more differentiated scheme (adapted model). More schools are now enjoying the challenges and rewards offered to all children in the competitive and co-operative models which are also included here.

Schools will choose events and activities best suited to their children, and which best meet the aims outlined above. Whichever model of organisation is chosen, it is a good idea to involve children in the planning process, for it will help them understand the principles involved in the event and to give them an opportunity to share their ideas, needs and concerns.

The traditional model

The traditional model of sports day is that of many people watching a few children competing in a succession of events, such as running, skipping, egg and spoon, sack, relays, etc. Sometimes children are allowed to enter a number of events, sometimes only one event. Races are often divided into boys' or girls' events, and banded acccording to age or year group. Some sports activities, like jumping or throwing, are often ignored. There is usually one race at a time; races are often organised in heats, and then finals, with points or prizes for the winners, and perhaps a trophy for the best team or house. Parents' or toddlers' races may add interest to the occasion. Little account is taken of the special needs of individual children, and only a few children are active at any one time.

Traditional model – adapted

Many schools have adapted this traditional model to include a wider variety of events such as ball, hoop or beanbag events, jumping and throwing events, mixed-age events, more team events and fun events such as wellie throwing, giant ball or space hopper races. It may be organised without points scored, or every child who enters scores so that all achieve some success. A wider variety of events allows for more differentiated activities and a wider range of sports experience, but this model continues the race/spectate tradition where most children remain, not active participants, but spectators.

The following models embody more successfully the principles of active PE by keeping all children active in a variety of events.

Active PE models

Active sports days embody the principle of keeping every child as active as possible in a variety of events that suit their needs. The sports area is divided into a number of stations (or events), and children rotate in groups around the circuit to each activity in turn. One teacher or adult helper is in charge of each station, with other helpers as needed. The circuit also includes opportunities for children to rest, and to have refreshments as appropriate. This approach aims to value the contribution of all children, not just the best athletes. Active sports days can be either competitive or co-operative, as in the following examples:

Competition model

The sports field is divided into ten activity areas, including two rest areas (figure 27). These activities can be adapted or varied to suit the needs and ages of the children. The competition is organised between four teams (or houses), each with a different colour; each event involves four children from each competing team. These teams can be single or mixed sex, but should be grouped by age or ability to allow for fair competition. This example will involve ten groups of 16 children (divided into four competing teams of four children).

Events happen simultaneously, and groups rotate to the next event every six to eight minutes (allowing two minutes' practice time) on a given signal. Each team group carries a scorecard to each station, and is given a score for each event. An example of scoring would be four points for the winner, three points for second, two points for third and one point for each other competitor. The competition is between teams rather than individuals, and as all score for each event, there will be an overall winning team or house, and ten winning teams (each of four children). All children are involved for most of the time (which helps with positive behaviour), and spectators are free to watch from several areas.

In addition to these events, sports day may include other special races such as mothers/toddlers, or relays for all to watch. Throwing and jumping events may be included, or held on another day, with two or four children per team. Instead of individual winning scores, a team score can be aggregated to find the winning team for each event. A recorder tallies the team scores, and special awards can be given to the winning team or to individuals for effort, improvement, co-operation, etc.

Fig 27: Competition model

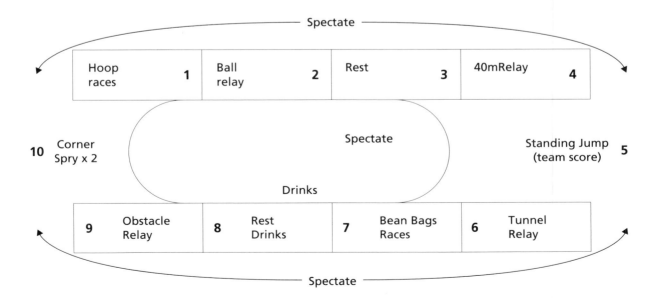

Co-operation model

This example shows 12 activity areas, including two rest areas (figure 28). Teams can be vertically grouped, for example with two or three children from each year, and 8 – 12 in a team. If infants and juniors are taking part they could be organised into six junior and six infant groups. Activities can be adapted accordingly to suit infants or juniors, as children progress around the circuit. Teams work together, encouraging each other to achieve a team score. A team leader takes a scorecard to each event, and points are awarded to teams rather than individuals. Awards can be given to the best team, the most co-operative team/individual, for good behaviour, etc. The events included in the diagram are:

1. 8 legged or 2x4 legged race: children in teams of two or four have legs tied, and are timed in making their way round cones or obstacle (two mats) course and back to start. Time both teams. Aggregate scores.
2. Obstacle course: under, over or through obstacle course, eg net, bench, barrel, hoop, etc. Time each team. Aggregate scores.
3. Sitting throw: with a football. Measure distance, aggregate team scores.
4. Hockey or football dribble: number two in team starts when number one is halfway round, etc. How far can the team go in two minutes?

Fig 28: Co-operation model

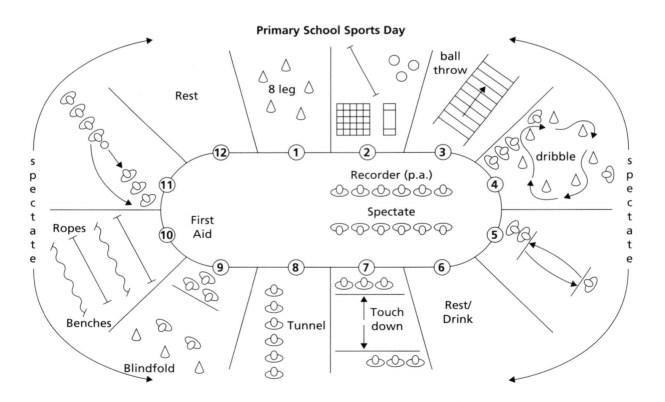

5. Shuttle relay: 30 metres (timed); allow several attempts for the best time.

6. Rest/drink.

7. Touchdown: using rugby ball or beanbag. Number one sprints with ball/beanbag to touchdown line and touches number two who repeats. How many team touchdowns in two minutes?

8. Tunnel race: through legs, race twice. Best time for the team?

9. Blindfold course: team calls instructions to one or two blindfold members to guide them round an obstacle course. All take turns (if possible); count how many successes in four or five minutes.

10. Over and under: a crossbar or bench, twice. Best time for team?

11. Bowl the hoop: to team member in a shuttle relay; join rear of group until all have had a turn. Try twice, best time for team.

12. Rest.

End of the Sports can include competitive relays and parents' races as appropriate.

Checklist for sports day
The following is a checklist of aspects of organisation for a sports day. These suggestions will need to be adapted to suit your circumstances. Whole staff planning and the involvement of children should help ensure a happy, active and successful sports day.

Half-term before
- plan the programme of events;
- plan staff/helper responsibilities;
- send out invitations/information to parents and other guests;
- check PA system (if needed);
- check markings on field (if needed);
- compile list of equipment needed;
- organise teams and entries;
- devise a wet-weather plan;
- include teaching for events in PE lessons;
- hold any extra events, eg jumping/throwing.

One week before
- send parents an information letter;
- confirm teacher/helper duties;
- display field plan for the sports day;
- agree rules for the day;
- teams chosen and practising (if possible);
- prepare recording/scoring procedures;

- plan refreshments;
- organise teams of helpers, eg for when sports are over.

On sports day
- check list of children/teams/helpers;
- prepare field for events;
- check first-aid;
- organise recording and scorecards;
- prepare refreshments;
- check field for stones, waste, etc;
- ensure children are ready changed and have been to the toilet!

After sports day
- thank helpers;
- give awards and praise;
- organise helpers to clear away apparatus;
- clear site of litter;
- review the day with staff/children involved.

Assessment

Children with special needs (see also p181).
Athletics provides opportunities for all children, including those with special needs, to become involved in a health-related fitness programme. However, special care must be taken to ensure the health and safety of children who have physical impairments: those prone to breathing problems, such as asthma, will need to be monitored closely for any signs of breathing difficulties.

Most children with special needs will want to participate at their level, and can be helped to set personal targets to encourage fitness and a sense of success. Children who are physically handicapped will often excel at certain physical activities, whether wheelchair or non-wheelchair events. Advice should be taken from parents and medical authorities, but wherever possible, they should participate in the activities of the lesson.

Assessment (see also pp169, 172)

There are different ways to approach the assessment of athletics. These include:

- Children's self-assessment: matching and recording their performance against their own best efforts.
- Teacher assessment records: recording the performances of individual children, and noting the achievements of each child.
- Athletic awards: participating in an award scheme and recording the progress of children according to a published table of achievements.

To assess and evaluate children's progress in athletics, it is probably best to use a performance table produced by one of the organsations that promote athletics awards for primary children, such as the Ten Step Award Scheme or the ESAA Award Scheme (see p189 for addresses). These schemes provide tables with sets of graded performances for children of all ablities.

What to look for

In assessing achievement in athletics, look for style and technique, not just performance, for example:

- Sprinting: speed of starting, straight running.
- Distance running: ability to jog/run up to given distance (eg 800 m– 1 km) continuously, with perseverence and determination.
- Jumping: spring, lift; safe and controlled landing.
- Throwing (ball): sideways on approach, fast action; power through use of body.
- Fitness: ability to repeat a sequence of fitness exercises; run continuously up to 1 km.
- Attitude: determination, perseverance, keenness, co-operation, fair play.

Swimming

'I'd love swimming if the water wasn't so wet!' *(junior child)*

By seven years old children will have varying degrees of experience and ability in swimming gained in and out of school. The aim of the National Curriculum is that at the end of Key Stage 2 'all pupils should be able to swim unaided at least 25 m and demonstrate an understanding of water safety'. This means that in schools where swimming opportunities are limited, priority will need to be given to non-swimmers and beginners. Ideally, a swimming programme will ensure that all children develop skill and confidence in swimming and diving techniques, as well as in water safety and survival.

This section on swimming provides a guide to the following:
• What to teach
• Lesson planning
• Gaining water confidence
• Stroke development
• Survival skills
• Swimming galas.

What to teach — swimming in the National Curriculum

The Progamme of Study for Key Stage 2 states that children should:

• learn and know the codes of hygiene and courtesy for using swimming pools;
• be given opportunities to develop confidence in water, be taught how to rest in water, how to float and to adopt support positions;
• be taught a variety of means of propulsion using either arms or legs or both, and develop effective and efficient swimming strokes on front and back;
• be taught water safety and the principles of water safety to assess the nature, visibility and location of water hazards in a variety of conditions;
• learn universal skills appropriate to their competence in water and evaluate their own abilities and limitations;
• be encouraged to assess their swimming and waterskills efficiency against a range of activities;
• explore the elements of movement in the water through simple games;
• be made aware of the role of swimming and water safety skills in supporting other water-based activities and activities near water.

(PE in the National Curriculum, 1992)

To meet the Attainment Targets and requirements for the Programme of Study for Key Stage 2, a swimming programme for primary children should include the following:

- learning about swimming (rules of hygiene, courtesy and safety at the pool);
- gaining water confidence (games and actitvities);
- learning to swim (learner pool activities);
- swimming stroke development (improving swimming styles);
- diving (getting in and out of the water);
- water survival (water safety hazards and activities);
- assessing progress in swimming (records of achievement).

Resources needed for swimming in the primary school include access to a learner pool, containing both shallow and deep water; buoyancy aids, including a variety of balls, rings and shapes, as well as inflatable arm bands and rings which are of suitable size and a comfortable fit for your children, and sufficient floatboards for each child to use, if needed. It is also useful to have a supply of extra swimming caps. Other useful equipment for teaching swimming and diving includes diving bricks, hoops (and weighted stands), diving discs, weighted toys, and light plastic balls.

The most valuable resources for swimming are of course the adult helpers: teachers, qualified swimming instructors and lifeguards. Very timid or physically disabled children may need an additional adult in the water. Swimming should be taught by a qualified swimming teacher. Local authority pool staff are often excellent swimming teachers; work with them to acquaint them with the Programme of Study for your children's individual needs. Teaching qualifications needed usually include the ASA preliminary teacher's award, and the bronze RLSS lifesaving award. Check at your local pool or with your LEA PE adviser or sports development officer for more information on ways to achieve these awards. Even if you are not a qualified swimming teacher, pool instructors may still welcome your help at the poolside.

Lesson planning

Whatever your access to swimming facilities, whether your own school pool, a pool at another school, or a local authority pool, early planning is advisable. Most schools will plan their programmes of swimming a year in advance, so that a pool is booked, curriculum time set aside and travel and transport arranged (perhaps parents can deliver or collect children, thus saving transport costs?).

Swimming lessons are often best arranged for the beginning or end of a school session so that they do not eat into other curriculum time.

Swimming lessons should be blocked over short, but intensive periods of time, so that continuity and progress can be maintained; for example in six or 12 once-a-week sessions.

Who should go swimming, and when? Which children should go swimming, and in which school year, will depend upon agreed school policies for swimming, and the availability of teaching facilities and personnel. Ideally, children should take part regularly in swimming throughout Years 3 – 6, whether they are non-swimmers, weak or strong swimmers. However, with the requirement that all children should learn to swim 25 metres and be taught water safety, the first priority in allocating swimming time should be to teach all children to swim, and this should be as early as possible, for example in Year 3.

Usually in a junior class there will be non-swimmers, beginner swimmers (able to swim up to 25 metres) and advanced swimmers (able to swim competently 25 metres or more on front and back). If pool time is limited, non- and beginner swimmers should be given a regular course of lessons, and opportunities found, if possible, for advanced swimmers to extend their skills and experience.

It is best to group children according to ability when teaching swimming; for example, in groups of non-swimmers, beginner swimmers and advanced swimmers. The following lesson plan is a framework that can be used or adapted for teaching children to swim in groups of any ability:

Before the lesson
- Register children and check on swimming gear.
- Discuss and agree rules of behaviour for travel, and procedures for changing.
- Remind children about the rules of safety and conduct in the water.

During the lesson
- Supervise water entry and introductory activities and games.
- Demonstrate, or instruct in swimming techniques.
- Active swimming practice (individual, group or class) and skills teaching.
- Time to practise individual skills or water games.

After the lesson
- Praise good effort and helpful behaviour.
- Assess and record progress.
- Present awards or certificates (if appropriate).

Aim for active and vigorous activity for most of the swimming lesson and ensure that all children know about codes of conduct and courtesy. Adopt a 'plan, perform and review' approach to activities; focus not only on effectiveness of mobility, but also on inventive and creative movement in water. Pacing is most important; try to ensure variety in activity and differentiation to suit individual needs. The aim is for children to enjoy a successful water experience, and to be able to meet realistic targets. Children like and respond best to teachers who are firm and businesslike in their approach; patient with individuals but keep children active; clear in their instructions and positive in their praise of effort or accomplishment.

Part of this businesslike approach is to be well prepared for the lesson, for example having armbands, floats, etc available at key points by the poolside before you begin. Safety is the prime concern, so before the lesson, ensure that a life-saver (if not you) is on active duty, and that any safety bar or harness that may be needed is available. Make sure you know emergency and life-saving procedures, in case of accident. Stand in a position where you are able to see all your pupils in and around the pool (see figures 29 – 31), and make sure that they know that they may enter the water only on your instruction.

Figs 29 – 31: Positions to stand by the poolside

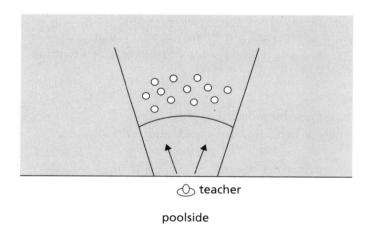

teacher

poolside

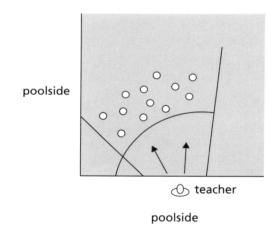

poolside

teacher

poolside

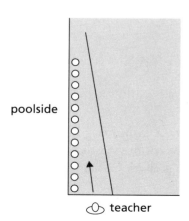

poolside

teacher

The teacher should stay out of the pool when responsible for, and teaching, the group; it is much easier to observe all the children from the poolside. Maintain firm discipline in and out of water. Train the children to respond quickly to your signal of 'Stop!', 'Listen!' or 'Out of the water!' (use a whistle if appropriate, and certainly to gain attention if it is a matter of safety). It is advisable to keep the group to a maximum of 20 children (12 or fewer is better).

Be patient in your approach and don't rush children who are lacking in confidence. Allow time to give individual help, allowing the most timid to sit and watch others if it helps build their confidence. When teaching, keep your instructions brief and simple and insist on silence and full attention when you speak. Use a clear signal for gaining attention and silence. If you are demonstrating a movement at the poolside, do it with dramatic expression, making sure that all can see and understand what you mean.

Learning about swimming

Learning about swimming can begin in the classroom through the use of books, pictures and posters. Involve children in helping to make up rules for hygiene, conduct, and safety at the poolside, and display them on bright charts as reminders, both in the classroom and at the poolside.
Rules could include:

- Help and care for each other.
- Change tidily and quickly.
- Use quiet voices.
- Walk: don't run or push.
- No outdoor shoes to be worn at the poolside.
- Clean feet, and go to the toilet before swimming.
- No chewing or eating beforehand.
- Have a clean towel and costume.
- Wear a swim hat if your hair is long.

Children suffering with heavy colds, catarrh or open sores should be excluded from the swimming lesson. Children with veruccas may wear verucca socks to protect against the spread of infection, though opinion about this differs widely.

Gaining water confidence

The key to teaching non-swimmers and beginners is to build their water confidence. This starts with entry into the water; it is important that the teacher or helper is present at the poolside to help give children confidence and to be sensitive to their needs.

Learner pool activities

The learner pool (see figure 32) should ideally be about 35 – 45 cm in depth, with steps into the water along the whole length of the pool.

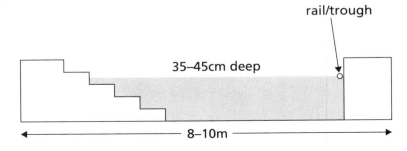

rail/trough

35–45cm deep

Fig 32: Diagram of learner pool

8–10m

Water entry

To help children enter the water, begin by letting them sit on the poolside, and gently move and kick their feet through the water. When confident at this, repeat the process on a lower step and gradually move down the steps, and deeper into the water. Practise stepping in and out of the water, deeper each time (first the ankles, then the knees, then the bottom, etc). As confidence grows, try walking into the water down the steps, holding hands with a partner already in the water, or holding a rail near the wall and walking down the steps into the water with your back to the water. For direct entry, sit on the poolside (not on the steps), place hands to one side, turn the body to lower yourself gently into the water. Ask children to find their own way to lower their body into the water, safely and slowly.

Water confidence

The following are some ways of developing water confidence:

- Wet your body all over with your hands, then splash water all over your body.
- 'Wash' your face in the water; pretend to take a bath or a shower (with hands cupped, drop water over your head).
- Standing or sitting, splash water all over yourself. Fingers open or closed? Which is best?
- Bend your knees; lower bottom, chest and shoulders under the water. First hold the rail or partner, then try without support.
- Bob up and down in the water, by yourself or holding a partner.
- Try to sit or kneel on the pool bottom. Which parts of your body can touch the bottom?
- Practise balancing on one leg, on one hand and one leg, and then the other leg, in the water.
- Try other water gymnastics, eg explore different shapes in the water (see Gymnastics pp30–31).
- Walk holding rail or trough around the edge of pool. On signal change direction or make a body shape.
- Walk, holding the rail as above, with your shoulders under water.
- Walk across the pool with, and then without, a partner (holding hands).
- Find other ways to move across the pool on your feet (eg hopping, jumping, sideways, backwards).
- Play freely with one of the floating shapes or aids: find ways to hold it and take one or both feet off the bottom.

Water games for gaining confidence

The following are some games to play in the water to help children gain water confidence. They can be adapted or developed according to the needs of the pupils:

Boats

A team of five or six children stand in line. Each child holds the shoulders or waist of the child in front. When ready, the leader walks into spaces in the water, leading the 'boat' of children linked together in line. Change leaders on signal. Can the 'boat' move backwards?

Simon says

Children repeat the teacher's actions at the poolside. All start with five points; no one drops out if they don't repeat the right action, but they lose a point through a false move.

Lifeboats

Teacher names the sides of the pool as parts of a boat, or points to the direction of travel. Children walk, run, hop or jump to the side indicated by the teacher. If 'lifeboat!' is called, children jump up, or go under water, or jump on the spot (or perform another given task).

Saved

The pool is scattered with various floats or swimming aids. Children may move freely about the pool; on a signal, children grab the nearest float to help them move to the nearest aid, or they must find a float of special shape or colour to 'save' themselves with and reach safety.

Splash! Splosh!

Children stand in two lines, back to back, one to two metres apart. One line is the Splashes, the other line is the Sploshes. On teacher's shout of 'Splash!' or 'Splosh!' the line called moves quickly to the side rail before other line can turn and catch them.

Beachcomber

Teacher scatters the pool with floats or swimming aids. Working together, children must collect as many floats, aids, etc from the surface, one at a time, to place on the poolside at the teacher's feet (eg in a basket). Teacher keeps count and can toss floats back into the water when a given time (say 30 seconds) is up.

Pearldiver

This game is similar to Beachcomber, but sinking objects (coins, spoons) are used for children to retrieve from the bottom of the pool.

Tag games

- **Touch:** child wearing armbands moves across the pool to touch as many others as possible. On a signal, eg a whistle, the last one touched becomes the next chaser. Children lose a life when tagged rather than drop out of the game.

- **Release:** chaser(s) wearing arm band chases and freezes tagged children, who in turn can be released with a touch from a releaser wearing two armbands (when more confident, release can be by touching a foot or moving through legs).
- **Chain:** chaser joins hands with tagged players. When four are tagged, children divide into pairs and so on.

Basking whales

Two or three children blow bubbles in the centre of the pool. Children try to cross to the other side. On a given signal whales tag the crossing children, who can escape by reaching or touching the opposite rail or a floating object thrown in the water.

Crafty captain

Children (the crew) line up at opposite end of pool to the teacher (the 'crafty captain in his/her cabin'), back facing the class. Children walk, shoulders under the water, until the 'captain' suddenly turns round to try to catch (see) anyone moving, or with their shoulders out of the water. 'Caught' crew take two or three paces back before restarting, and trying to reach the captain's cabin. How many can reach the cabin in set time?

Chanting games

Rhymes such as 'Ring o' roses', 'Pop goes the weasel' are excellent played in a circle. Children, hands joined, walk round singing or chanting. On the punch lines 'All fall down!' or 'Pop goes the weasel!' the children can submerge, jump up high, sit on bottom, etc depending on confidence or ability.

Invent other games, singing songs you know, moving through and ducking under the water. Singing can help calm nervous children – and teachers!

Pair activities for water confidence

Simple activities might include:

- **Follow the leader:** no holding, copying the leader's actions. Practice wading, knees bent, pulling the water back with hands.
- **Crossing:** cross from opposite ends; at the centre perform a pair action (eg clap hands; jump up and down alternately, holding hands; pass over and under each other) then continue to the other side.
- **Chase the leader:** on signal, both stop; chaser attempts to touch the leader.
- **Pair race:** pairs hold hands or hold round each other's waists. On signal, cross pool using free arms to propel forward.
- **Jack-in-the-box:** pairs hold hands and alternately bend knees for shoulders under, then heads under (remember to take a deep breath each time!).

- **Pair passing:** using a ball, a quoit, and a float; children stand back-to-back and pass object over heads and between legs, alternately.
- **Hoops:** in pairs. Find different ways to pass through a hoop: a) held vertically under the surface; b) horizontally on the surface. How many can you perform in 30 seconds?

Learning to swim

After water confidence has been gained through a variety of confidence-building activities, learning to swim can begin in easy stages, slowly improving with practice:

Shallow water: propulsion

Swimming depends on propelling the body through water. The shallow water in a learner pool is ideal for practising exercises in propulsion through water:

- Practise pushing water backwards by moving the palms of your hands downwards and sideways.
- Practise pushing water downwards and forwards with your hands.
- Practise crouch walking: shoulders under water, using hands to pull and push while moving: a) forwards; b) backwards (demonstrate hand movements from the poolside).
- Ensure children can touch pool bottom with hands easily and try: a) crawling on hands and knees; b) moving on hands and both feet, then one foot, taking the other foot off the bottom every so often; c) walking on hands, with body in a prone (front) position; legs out straight, keeping chin on the surface of the water; d) walking on hands, with body in a supine (back) position; legs out straight, keeping chin on the surface of the water.

Breathing: introductory activities

One of the problems to overcome in learning to swim is how to breathe in water. Build up confidence in breathing in and under water by:

- Blowing objects through the water, eg table tennis balls, to a partner.
- Cup hands full of water; put your lips to the water and blow hard.
- Hold rail: bend knees, take a deep breath; eyes closed, put your head under and blow bubbles.
- Try the above with your hands on the bottom of the shallow pool.
- Try putting your head under the water, with eyes open, and count the fingers shown by a partner.
- With head under, as above, can you hum or make noises under water?

- Free-standing in the water: deep breath, head under, blow bubbles, come up for air; repeat several times.
- Make different shapes, eg curl/stretch/twist, in the water. What shapes can you make? Which help you float in water?

More propulsion activities

These activities are suitable for deeper water, such as the shallow end of a main pool, in a roped-off area for safety:

- Walk children around the activity area, with the water never more than chest high.
- Children hold rail, make waves with chest and shoulders, moving forwards and backwards.
- Release rail, make waves by sweeping arms, palms leading; forwards and backwards.
- Walk, sliding feet along the bottom; pull back water with palms.
- Practise being wading ducks, leaping frogs, crocodiles, dolphins, etc, with suitable actions to encourage: shoulders under; wet faces; pushing down and pulling back with palms; one foot then both feet off the bottom; forward movement.
- Facing rail, two metres from the side: lean forward, bend knees and push off to reach for the rail.
- Stand further back from the rail, push off and glide to rail; increase distance as confidence grows.

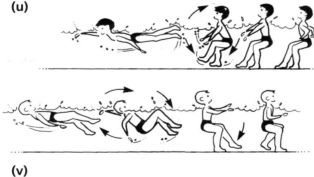

(u)

(v)

- Practise recovery from a prone position (u): lean forwards to lay on the water; lift your head, tuck up your knees and lift your feet off the bottom. Pull palms down and move them to and fro in the water; recover by dropping your feet to the pool floor.
- Practise recovery from a supine position (v): lay back in the water; pull your arms down and backwards, lift head, lift knees up towards chest, lower feet to floor as arms move forward and out to keep balance and aid recovery position.

Note: some children might prefer to twist and rotate sideways, lifting head and opposite shoulder to regain standing position.

Swimming aids

Swimming aids, such as inflatable armbands, floats and rings, can be used to help give children confidence, to maintain their buoyancy and achieve the correct hoizontal body positions. Some costumes may have pockets to house floats around the waist.

(w)

The use of inflatable armbands and waist-bands allows children to dog paddle and use swimming arm actions while kicking legs. A rope supporting a flat rubber ring can support a child while swimming when held from the side by a teacher. Support using rope and ring can be decreased gradually (w).

Use armbands, waist-bands and rings in addition to or instead of floats as required. Children will vary in their needs. Activities using buoyancy and swimming aids include:

- Hold floats under each arm; hop on one leg, then the other, to push clear of pool floor.
- Hold floats as above, and frog kick or scissor-kick.
- Hold floats to your tummy and push off floor to make different body shapes: tuck/stretch (arched), star shapes, etc.
- Hold float(s) with arms outstretched; lean forward, and hop on one foot.
- Hold floats as above and glide to rail or a partner from a one-leg push.
- On your front. Hold a float with arms outstretched; scissor-kick across pool.
- Hold float as above and frog-leg across pool.
- On your back. Hold a float under each arm (or hold close to chest) then push off from wall to partner, standing one or two metres away (increase distance as confidence grows).
- On your back as above and either scissor-kicks or frog-leg kick across pool.

Partner towing for beginners

In prone position. Hold your partner's hands or shoulders (xi – ii); partner tows you, as you lay on the surface with arms outstretched, across the pool. Vary with leg kick action.

(xi)   **(xii)**

Wheelbarrow

A supporting partner stands between the swimmer's straddled legs to support the hips. Swimmer uses arms for dog paddle, sculling, or swimming with arm stroke across the pool on front or back (yi – ii).

(yi)   **(yii)**

Shoulder support

In supine position. Support your partner's shoulders as s/he scissor-kicks or frog-legs across pool on back, holding tummy high, and head back, with arms sculling at the side (z).

(z)

Stroke development

When children are water confident, buoyant and begin to move through the water confidently, they can begin to learn the major strokes: back crawl, front crawl, breast stroke and survival strokes. Although children cannot learn all the strokes at once, it is good to teach them to swim on front and back from the beginning. Many children find backcrawl appealing because of ease of breathing.

There are three basic ways of teaching stroke development:

- **The 'part-stroke' method**, where parts of a stroke are practised in isolation, then linked together until the whole stroke is practised, eg front crawl legs, arms, then whole stroke; add breathing technique as progress is made.
- **The 'whole-part-whole' method**, where the whole stroke is practised, then parts of the stroke are practised in isolation before the whole stroke is practised again (with or without swimming aids).
- **The 'whole-stroke' method**, more suitable for advanced swimmers; the whole stroke is practised but the child concentrates on a special aspect, such as explosive breathing or hand entry, while performing the whole movement.

Classes can usually be divided into three ability groups: beginners and non-swimmers; improvers – able to swim one or two widths on front or back; and advanced – able to swim 25 m on front and back and tread water in deep end of the pool.

Children should sometimes have the opportunity of seeing others swim before trying for themselves. In teaching stroke development, remember to try both 'part' and 'whole-part-whole' approaches. Advanced swimmers should be trained in whole movements, with a focus on improving a particular element of their style. Introduction to simple watermanship and survival skills should form part of all lessons, as they are important and can add variety and fun to a stroke-development lesson. Advanced swimming techniques can be followed in the ASA and STA handbooks (see Resources p189) or see the ASA's *Swimming Teaching and Coaching Level 1* and *Handbook for the Teacher of Swimming* (Pelham Books).

The following are some suggestions for developing the four major swimming strokes :

Back crawl

Main teaching points:

- Body position: lay supine in the water; look up, hold your tummy up and hips high.
- Legs: kick from the hips about 30 cm deep; stretch toes; whip them in a continuous scissor action.

Fig aa: Back crawl from side and front

- Arms (entry and pull): keep your arms straight when reaching beyond your head; little finger should enter the water first; palm out, pulling sideways with nearly straight arm on recovery; keep the arm straight by your side, lift hand up and reach back with a straight arm to repeat the action.
- Breathing: breath rhythmically, breathing in as one arm recovers, and out as the other recovers.
- Timing: try to achieve three or six kicks to every arm cycle.

Introducing the back crawl

- Practise recovering to a standing position from a back glide (with partner supporting shoulders if necessary).
- Holding the rail. Practise holding a tuck position on the wall, then push back in a glide position to partner's arms.
- Practise as above, with a float held: a) to the chest (bbi); or b) under head (bbii); or c) extended beyond head (bbiii), then scissor-kick feet to float across the pool or to a partner.

Fig bb i–iii: Gliding on back with float

(bbi)   **(bbii)**

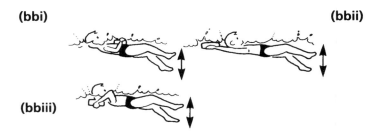

(bbiii)

When children are confident in these backstroke exercises, then gliding on the back can be tried without a float, using a sculling action with the hands. Demonstrate the arm action from the side of the pool, or when all are out of the pool, watch a good backstroke swimmer in the water. Ways of practising the arm strokes include:

- Hook feet under the pool rail, in a supine position, and practise arm movements (easier).
- Straddle the legs, with partner supporting the hips, and then practise arm stroke (see wheelbarrow p133).
- Grip a float between the thighs (or tuck in costume around waist) and practise arm movements only, then the whole stroke.
- See how many strokes each child can make and how far they can go in the water without support.

Breast stroke

Fig cc: Breast stroke

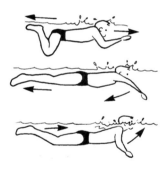

Main teaching points:

- **Body position:** lie on the water in a prone position, looking forwards and downwards, legs straight and together.
- **Legs:** bend knees, point feet towards the pool bottom; heels together, turn feet outwards, heels ready to drive out and back; sweep legs round and together; kick back and together.
- **Arms** (pull): arms outstretched in a glide position; pull outwards and down and backwards, keeping arms straight until just before shoulder line.
- **Arms** (recovery): bend arms and bring to chin smoothly; elbows tucked in, arms stretched out forward to glide position.
- **Breathing:** breathe in during pull, breathe out as arms stretch forward (blowing your hands away from you).
- **Timing:** pull and breathe in; kick, glide and breathe out.

Introducing the breast stroke

- Demonstrate the arm stroke from side of the pool, then leg stroke (a competent swimmer can do this lying on a table or when lying prone on the poolside).
- Watch a demonstration by a good swimmer in the water, performing the whole stroke.
- Push off and glide in prone position; attempt the whole stroke.
- Stand in the water, keeping shoulders under, and practise arm action.
- Practise as above, walking across the pool.
- Practise the leg action, holding rail and pushing against wall, in prone position (knees up, heels together and towards pool bottom; feet turned out, kick with soles of feet and inner part of legs).
- Push off from the side and glide; practise two or three leg kicks.
- Practise as above, with a float, moving across the pool.

- Push off and glide, one arm pull, one leg kick.
- Increase the number of strokes, striving for timing and rhythm: pull and breathe, kick, glide and blow out.

Front crawl

Main teaching points:

- **Body position:** prone, looking down and forward (not breathing) and sideways (breathing).
- **Legs:** kick from the hips, 30 cm deep; slight knee bend, with long legs and pointed toes.
- **Arms** (entry): keep arms straight beyond your head, fingers in first and together; pull water, keeping elbow up; push and straighten arm.
- **Arms** (recovery): swing elbow up and forward; reach forward with hand.
- **Breathing:** head must be turned sideways to breathe, as one arm begins pull and the one on breathing side completes; push breath out forcefully as face is submerged.
- **Timing:** keep kicking throughout the arm cycle.

Introducing the front crawl

- Demonstrate use of arms from the poolside, or watch a good swimmer in the water.
- Push off from the side into a front glide position; hold breath, put face in the water.
- Practise as above, holding float in outstretched arms; glide and scissor kick.
- Practise as above, kicking from hips to refine the leg action (flipper feet!).
- One hand holding the rail, one pushed against the wall to hold a prone position; practise leg kick (see previous points).
- With float, kick across the pool, face in the water; breathe quickly in front, breathe out slowly with face in water.
- Practise arm movements and breathing again (see above teaching points).
- Keeping shoulders under water, copy the front crawl action, then try with face in the water.
- Practise as above, with face in water, walking across pool.
- Push off from the side in front glide; kick legs and practise arm action.

Fig dd: Front crawl

- Push off; with face in the water, practise leg kick and arm action together. How many strokes can you achieve? How far can you go in one breath?
- Holding rail and wall, practise leg kick and turning head to breathe; increase number of breaths. Blow out hard and long, breathe in quickly.
- Practise the whole stroke: face in water, hold breath for three to four strokes, then turn face to breathe.
- Practise as above, increasing number of breaths until one breath for every arm cycle.

The **butterfly stroke** is an advanced stroke that can be introduced after the other strokes have been well learnt. It is not necessary to learn the butterfly stroke for water safety purposes. For further information on this stroke refer to the handbooks mentioned previously.

Diving

Improver and advanced swimmers should be introduced to a number of ways of entering the water, including standard diving procedures. Children find the different ways of entering the water very exciting, offering plenty of scope for imagination and invention. As a preliminary to diving, children should practise a variety of underwater movements, such as:

- keeping their eyes open under water;
- springing from standing on the pool floor (with water at chest depth) to diving, rolling, and performing other water stunts;
- trying a variety of ways of gliding and swimming under water;
- standing in their depth of water, practising water gymnastics, handstands, somersaults, etc;
- kneeling, sitting, and lying on the pool floor in the deepest water they can.

Diving feet first
Try making a variety of dives, starting from a standing position, such as:

- Pencil dive: step or jump, arms at side, legs together on entry (eei) (when confident, try this raising arms straight abovethe head (ii)).
- Spring to make a shape in the air (tuck, long, wide) before entering with feet together.
- Straddle entry into shallow water: feet forward and back, arms forward and sideways, keeping head dry.
- Spring jump: tuck or sit in the air, and keep that position on entry into the water.
- Jump into a shape in the air; straighten, to enter with arms straight, above your head.

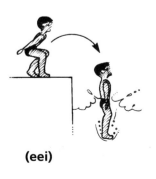
(eei)

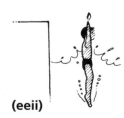
(eeii)

- Jump, to straddle legs; try to touch knees or ankles before entering as above.
- Find ways to jump, then twist with a quarter, half or full turn in the air before entering the water.
- Jump out and turn backwards to enter the water facing the rail.
- Create your own funny jumps, ensuring a safe water entry away from the edge of the pool.

Head-first diving

Here are some ways to practise diving into the water head first:

- **Crouching dive:** crouch roll in a tucked, rounded shape, toes gripping edge, chin on chest, holding ankles with hands; roll forward into water (ff).
- **Sitting dive:** sit with feet on rail, knees and feet together; arms straight, pressed close to ears, palms down and touching, chin on chest. Lean forward, lift hips, overbalance and push with feet to enter water, hands and feet first (keep chin on chest!) (gg).

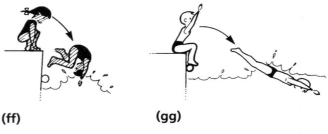

(ff)   **(gg)**

(hh)

- **Kneeling dive:** with one knee near the edge and toes of other foot gripping the edge; toes of rear leg curled ready to push off; arms straight, pressed close to ears; leaning forward, push with rear foot, chin near chest, legs extended, reach for the bottom of the pool (hh).
- **Low crouch dive:** as above, except start in crouch position on edge of pool, knees together and arms extended; push from both feet to reach towards the pool floor (ii).
- **High crouch dive:** as before, but knees only half bent, body leaning forward 45°; push outward and upward, through feet and lower body, to enter water fully stretched, head down and toes pointed (jj).

(ii)   **(jj)**

(kk)

- **Plunge dive:** feet slightly apart, toes gripping edge, and knees bent; keep the upper body horizontal, arms hanging down, and eyes looking forward into water; swing arms back and forward; extend ankles, knees and hips vigorously, to plunge dive. Try to maintain a horizontal, streamlined body position until you have entered the water. Enter shallow for front crawl and a quick return to the surface; enter in more depth for the breast or butterfly stroke, to allow one underwater stroke; enter more deeply for underwater swimming (kk).

Plain header dive

A plain header dive is similar to a high crouch dive, except that diver starts upright, in a Y standing position (legs straight, arms stretching out), lower body thrust upwards (this is crucial as the arms should remain above the head all through the movement), to enter the water as straight and as vertical as possible (ll).

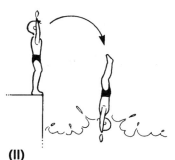

(ll)

Survival skills

Survival skills can be divided into floating, treading water, survival strokes, and getting in and out of the water. The following are some examples of basic survival skills and activities:

Floating

Floating can be a vital skill for conserving energy in water and where there may be hazards beneath the surface to prevent you treading water. Skills and activities include:

- **Supine floating:** lie on your back, holding hips high, keeping tummy up; extend the legs, keeping arms by the side or stretched out in a star position. Try to keep your face out of the water.
- **Prone floating:** lie face down in the water, arms and legs extended in the star position. Lift head to breathe, then lower head into the water again, breathing out slowly.
- **Vertical floating:** keep upright, with arms bent and hands at the side of your body (palms facing down into the water). Everything should be submerged except your head (chin resting on the surface). Tilt head back to breathe. If you begin to sink, then tread water!

Treading water

Maintain a vertical position in the water, using minimum arm and leg movements to keep afloat. Arms should scull sideways, moving away from and towards the body. Legs can either move downwards in breast stroke action, make a cycling movement, or a front crawl kick.

Using clothes as floats

Use some old, everyday items of clothing, such as pyjamas, shirts, or trousers, as floats to aid bouyancy and survival in water as in the following activities:

• Take an item of clothing into the water, find an opening, tie one end such as a trouser leg or sleeve end, wave the garment out of the water to trap air, and bring it down vigorously under water to form a float (with the trapped air).
• Blow into the garment, then tie or hold the openings closed to form a float.
• Practise in shallow water, then develop while treading water in the deep end of the pool.

Children can use floats under arms, under the head, or between their legs to float and help conserve energy. After these techniques have been practised, children can then try taking clothes off in the water, while treading water. Trousers are easiest to remove, then shirt or pyjama tops. Children can try to seal the openings of their clothes by tying them before trying to trap air inside them.

Survival strokes

Sculling with hands

Main teaching points:

• Lie on the surface of the water in a supine position, looking up, with arms moving smoothly in a flat figure of eight; keep the tummy and hips up, and legs together. Hands should be cupped, with palms turned away from the direction of travel and moved to scull the body along.
• Push off and glide, with hands pushing the water back (palms cupped).
• Practise as above, making a figure of eight movement with the arms.

Elementary backstroke

Main teaching points (mm):

• Lie on the water in a supine position, looking up.
• Keep legs and ankles together below the surface.
• Kick your heels down and back, turning feet out before each kick.
• Sweep lower legs round and together.

- Keep arms straight by the sides; slide palms up along body to stretch out in a V beyond the head, keeping arms under water.
- Sweep arms round and pull the water, keeping arms straight.
- Breathe in and recover arms, breathe out and pull and kick.
- Recover the arms and legs, then pull and kick together.

(mm): back stroke

Introducing the elementary backstroke
- Demonstrate with good swimmer in the water (class out of water).
- Push off from side on back, practising leg kick (hands can scull).
- Push off from side on back with float held on chest, practising leg kick.
- Push off from side and practise one or two arm pulls and leg kicks.

Sidestroke
Main teaching points:

- Lie on your side in the water, legs outstretched and together; bend and separate the legs.
- Make a scissor kick, straighten legs and repeat.
- Lower arm leads and stretches forward, upper arm lies stretched out along the body.
- Bend the lower arm, pull water back and stretch towards head.
- Recover and bend top arm close to the body, pressing palm down and back towards chest.
- Bend arms and legs (breathe in) part hands, pull and kick (breathe out).

Introducing the sidestroke
A useful way of demonstration is to watch a good swimmer swimming sidestroke in the water. Practise by pushing off and gliding on your side, with bottom arm leading, and with top arm pulling back and adding the scissor leg action.

Water safety and hazards

Getting in and out of the water

Children should be taught various ways of entering unknown waters, and be made aware of the possible presence of dangerous obstacles beneath the surface. The straddle jump or surface dive are useful alternative ways of entering the water. If entry can be gained by walking or wading, then this will often be the safest course.

(nn)

Getting in: the straddle jump

This will prevent the child sinking deeply into water, if the following points are practised and remembered:

- Jump out across the surface of the water.
- Stretch out arms and legs as wide as possible to make a big surface impact.
- Straddle legs, one forwards and one backwards.
- Jump with your body leaning slightly forwards (helps to keep your hair dry!).

Getting out

Getting out of water is not always as easy as it looks; try practising these points:

- swim to the side of the pool, placing hands on the side, one shoulder-width apart;
- push hard on hands to lie on tummy on pool edge (feet still in water);
- swing body sideways, bending one knee to place on the edge of the pool; the whole body can then be drawn alongside before standing position is regained.

Life saving

Children should be aware of hazards when participating in water-based activities or when near water. They need to be taught watchfulness, decision-making and what life-saving action to take.

Watchfulness

Things to watch for may include:

- A struggling swimmer.
- Someone disappearing and reappearing in water.
- Someone drifting out to sea or down river on an airbed, raft or canoe.
- Someone chasing a ball out to sea.
- Someone who has capsized a canoe or dinghy.

Decision-making

Discuss what to do if you see something potentially dangerous in or near the water: how to alert others, seek for help and to inform emergency services.

(oo)

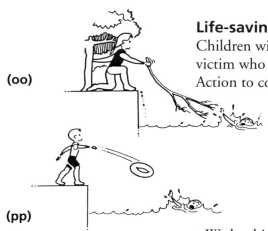

Life-saving action

Children will rarely be strong enough at this stage to swim and tow a victim who is in trouble in the water, but some action can be taken. Action to consider in discussing priorities might include:

- Reaching a victim from dry land: lie flat, hold on to something secure with one hand and grasp the victim with the other. Extend your reach by holding a branch, a rope, a pole or clothing (oo).
- Throwing an aid: anything that will float may provide buoyancy, eg a beachball, a ring, polystyrene. Allow for the influence of wind and currents (pp).

(pp)

- Wade: this extends the reach; wade up to the thighs, using a stick to test the depth before using hands or other materials to reach the victim. If more than one is rescuing, a chain can be formed, which will also extend the reach of one person.

- Row (if rescuer and a friend can handle a boat): approach slowly, stern first; instruct victim to hold the stern of the boat, and support him/her until help arrives. Alternatively, row to safety, or throw a rope or buoyancy aid from the boat (qq).
- Swim to take an aid: a lifebelt, rope or anything that will float. Physical contact with the victim must be avoided, but support can be thrown to assist a victim until help arrives (rr).

(qq)

(rr)

Resuscitation

Children should learn how to give mouth-to-mouth resuscitation; they should have expert instruction in this from a qualified life-saving teacher or St John's Ambulance personnel. The following are the basic principles of resuscitation:

- start resuscitation immediately, even in shallow water, if possible;
- lay the victim on their back; tilt head back, lifting the jaw (to clear tongue from throat);
- if breathing has not restarted clear the mouth of any blockage;
- pinch the victim's nose, cover it, and blow into the mouth at a rate of once approximately every five seconds.

Alternatively, cover the victim's mouth with one hand, then blow gently and firmly into their nose. Turn your head to take another breath and watch the victim's chest fall as breath is automatically exhaled.

Personal survival and safety skills are usually practised in a warm pool, but ideally children should experience some outdoor water-based activities, so that they can appreciate the dangers and difficulties first hand, while being safely supervised. A common problem is exposure, leading to hypothermia, which is recognised by extreme shivering and rigid muscles, leading to drowsiness and finally unconsciousness. People who are cold, wet and shivering need to be dried briskly, dressed, covered with warm blankets and given a warm drink.

Swimming activities and games

Activities and games (for the middle and deep ends of the pool) can provide:

- An introduction to more advanced swimming and water skills.
- A change from stroke development and practice.
- Fun, and the development of positive attitudes.

Individual activities include:

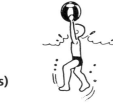

(ss)

(tt)

- **Bicycle:** tread water with breast stroke arms and cycling legs. Find other ways to keep upright, treading water, eg breast stroke legs; flutter kick; figure 8 with hands, etc.
- **Water walk:** tread water and try to 'walk' in different directions, keeping upright.
- **Hands up:** tread water with one or two hands held high; try holding a float or ball above your head (ss).
- **Sculling:** on the back, head first; wrists cocked back, fingers pointed up, palms pressed towards feet. Try sculling in different directions, eg feet first, altering the angle and position of hands, feet gently kicking. Then try hands moving only.
- **Spinning wheel:** scull while stationary; move into a tuck position, body tilted to one side. Lower arm makes flat, sculling action, while legs 'cycle' to cause rotation. Keep upper hand on hip, and elbow stuck out.
- **Canoe:** in a prone position, back arched, head and heels clear of surface; hands scull towards the feet from beside the hips to move forward, head first, like a canoe.
- **Mushroom:** float head down in a tucked position holding knees, with back protruding above the surface of the water. Hold your breath (underwater) for as long as possible before standing (shallow water) or treading water again (tt).
- **Drowned:** from a mushroom float position; extend arms and legs loosely and maintain head-down position, like a drowned person. Hold breath, then recover to tread water.
- **Underwater:** breast stroke underwater across the pool from a poolside dive or a push off from the side. How far/how many strokes can you swim underwater?

- **Search:** swim across the pool, duck dive at centre, pick up an object from the bottom, carry it close to chest using backstroke leg kicks.
- **Injured swim:** swim on front or back without using one arm, one leg, or arm and leg.
- **Rolling log:** combined front and back crawl. Right arm pulls for front crawl, roll on to back, left arm pulls for back crawl; repeat continuously.
- **Porpoise:** scull face down, dip head and lift legs for surface dive. Scull underwater then raise head, hollowing back, up to surface. Breathe, and repeat.
- **Propeller:** float on back, arms together stretched beyond your head; bend wrists, scull with palms pushing away from head, feet leading.
- **Floating letters:** make letter shapes Y, L, C, O, T, I with body while floating and sculling on front, side or back. Can you spell a word?
- **Forward somersault:** tread water, with arms sideways; tuck knees into chest, drop chin to chest, press arms downwards, forwards and upwards, lifting hips to somersault body.
- **Back somersault:** float on back, arms tucked in, palms down; tuck knees into chest, head pressed back, lift knees and push down with palms to rotate backwards.
- **Extended front somersault:** float on back; head back, hollow back, arms sweep forward and down as hips follow rotation. Try to keep legs together, knees slightly bent before resurfacing.

Encourage children to create and explore other individual skills and stunts in a free time for physical activity in the water.

Pair activities

Working with a partner can extend the range of physical activity in the water. The following are some pair activities to explore water and swimming skills:

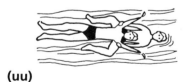

(uu)

- Leap frog: over partner's back or shoulders with a jump and dive in shallow water (no touching).
- Double breaststroke: with B gripping A's waist.
- Double backstroke: with A gripping B's shoulders (uu).
- Double front crawl: with A's legs around B's neck or waist.
- Double back crawl: with A's legs around B's neck or waist (vv).
  Can you find other ways to swim while linked together with a partner?

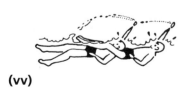

(vv)

- Tired swimmer: A on back, legs together, or in straddle shape, keeping arms straight. A grips B's shoulders, B swims breaststroke. Can you find other ways of swimming with a tired swimmer?
- Pair sculling: float position, both facing same way. B's feet grip A's neck; both scull together.
- Can you find other ways to scull while linked: a) in different directions; b) with different links?
- Follow your leader: B follows A swimming on or underwater; repeating stroke, floating or other actions in the water.

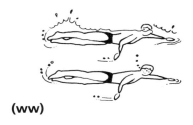

(ww)

(xx)

- Mirror image: A swims breaststroke on surface while B mirrors action underwater or on the surface. This can also be practised in threes or fours (ww).

Try these formations in threes, swimming breaststroke or backstroke to begin with:

- Triangle: A leads with B and C in line abreast.
- Line: all swim in line abreast, taking lead from A or C.
- File (in fours): swim behind each other, keeping equal spaces; swim in square or diamond formations.
- Sculling: A, B, C pointing head first, gripping each other's shoulders. A and C scull with hands; all kick legs to keep afloat (xx).

Large-group activities

There are many different ways that children can swim in formation; for example, children can help plan

- lines crossing in opposite directions, sculling or swimming;
- lines crossing, with one wave swimming under the other;
- criss-crossing using individual strokes or double-linked strokes.

Shallow-water games

More advanced swimmers will enjoy these too!

Horse and jockey

Pairs face each other in two circles, one inside the other. On signal, inside 'jockeys' surface dive through partner's ('horses') legs, swim round circle, then mount their horse's back.

Tunnels

Half the group are 'tunnels', half are 'divers'. Tunnels stand in ones, twos or threes, legs apart, hands on shoulders of those in front. Divers swim below as many tunnels as possible in a set time.

Numbers

Group treads water. On number being called (two to six), children in circle hold hands to form groups of that number.

Stuck on the bottom

Group spreads out in the water, with one, two or more as 'taggers'. On signal, they swim to tag (touch) as many as possible. Tagged players stand (in their depth) 'stuck on the bottom', or tread water. They can be released by being touched by free swimmers, or (to make it harder) only by free swimmers swimming between their legs.

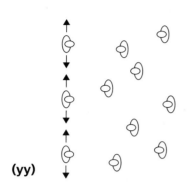

(yy)

Chinese wall

Two or three taggers stand or tread water in centre of pool. Group attempts to cross pool without being tagged. Taggers may only move sideways. Tagged players join taggers in a second line (yy).

Circle chase

In circles of five to twelve children, numbered odds and evens. On signal, children swim around circle and back to places. Extend by swimming through partner's legs before or after swimming around circle.

Ball toss

In small groups, treading water; children toss ball to each other to count consecutive passes before ball is dropped. One- or two-handed passes.

Ball spry

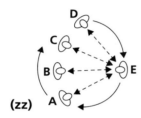

(zz)

E & D swim round team
after passes complete
A becomes feeder
E replaces A after circuit
D returns to place

In fours or fives, treading water. A faces the team, three or four metres away, and tosses ball to each in turn; next swimmer replaces A. Variations: a) one- or two-handed passes; b) thrower and last receiver swim round the team; the next player in line becomes the new thrower (zz).

Polo passes

Games of 3v1, 4v2, developing to 2v2, 3v3, 4v4. Players aim to make consecutive passes, avoiding interception or dropped pass (when the ball hits the water). When a game restarts, the opposing team obtains possession. Adjust depth of water and feet-on-floor contact to suit the swimmers' ability.

Red, amber, green

When colours are called, swimmers react quickly as follows:

• Red – floating or stationary sculling.
• Amber – treading water.
• Green – swimming freely, without touching each other.

Sinking plate

Class in circles, numbered, standing or treading water. One swimmer in centre of circle drops plastic plate or disc and calls out a number; that swimmer dives to retrieve plate before it touches the bottom.

Porpoise race

Teams of five or six, sculling side by side. On signal, swimmer A surface dives over B's legs, then under C's legs, over D's legs and so on (each takes a turn at being the porpoise).

Relays

Obstacle relays can be devised, in small teams of 3 or 4 and in water of suitable depth, such as shuttle relays with the following variations:

- Dribble balls, pass and swim after balls to reach swimmer on the opposite side of the pool.
- Pick up objects from pool bottom, pass to next swimmer who drops to bottom and touches next swimmer.
- Swim through hoops held under the surface.
- Surface diving, over and under ropes.

Other relays can be played in fours across the pool, such as:

- Float relay: kicking legs or arm action only.
- Injured relay: stroke restriction (eg immobilising an arm or leg).
- Carry relay: passing a float or ball when incoming swimmer touches the side of the pool (if a swimmer starts from each side simultaneously, each with a float or ball respectively, these can be exchanged at mid-point, then again on reaching the side).
- Dressing or undressing (wearing pyjama tops or bottoms). A, wearing top, dives in, swims across, climbs out, undresses, hands to B and so on (vary by dressing or undressing in the water in middle or side of pool).

For further ideas for games and activities refer to *Enjoy Swimming* (Faber & Faber), *Swimming Games and Activities* (A&C Black).

For Resources for swimming see p189.
For Assessment of swimming see pp169, 173

Swimming galas

A school swimming gala or open session of water activities to which parents and others are invited to watch, can provide a purpose and audience for all children involved in swimming. Such a gala can include many fun, team and novelty events, interspersed with the usual width and length races. Except for best swimmers, it is a good idea to make most events relays or team events (many children are fearful of individual, competitive swimming).

Beginner events (perhaps in a teaching pool) and swimmer events can take place simultaneously, and could include some activities demonstrating watermanship and survival skills; opportunities can be found for all children to take part. The following are some activities that could be included in a school or class swimming gala:

Beginner events
- Blow the balloon relay (across the pool).
- Dressing relay (shorts or tops).
- Over ropes or through the hoop relay.
- Collecting corks or floats to put into a basket.
- Collecting coins or spoons from the bottom of the pool.
- Float relay (holding float on front or back and kicking legs).
- Walking (shoulders under) relay.

Swimmer events
- Width and length races, according to ability or age.
- Width and length relays (mixed age).
- Diving displays (plain header, plunge diving).
- Sculling races (or team event).
- Pair races (or team event).
- Ball tossing/passing relays.
- Obstacle relays.
- Duck-diving for coins or spoons.
- Watermanship skills demonstration.

Shallow end (width) events and deep end (team) events can take place simultaneously. It may be advisable to hold individual length races and diving events at the beginning, and team length races at the end of the gala. This will keep most children active for most of the time, and keep spectators interested, whilst saving the excitement of the length races and relays for the climax of the gala.

Record of achievement and awards
Both the ASA and the STA have excellent award schemes for all levels of ability, from beginners to advanced, and personal survival awards. The RLSS also organises beginner awards suitable for older juniors (see Resources for addresses).

Planning a swimming gala

The following is a timetable for planning a swimming gala for one or more participating schools:

One year before
• Book the swimming pool.

One term before
• Develop and share ideas for the event with other staff.
• Devise plans for the gala with the children who will be involved.
• Advertise the event, eg in a school newsletter.
• Send out any special invitations, eg to governors.
• Check any pool requirements, eg the need for a PA system, lane markers, small apparatus.

Half a term before
• Plan events, activities, entries and or teams.
• Devise a programme order of events.
• Create a poster to advertise the event.
• Organise transport arrangements.
• Inform and invite parents and any other guests.

One week before
• Send parents final details of the event.
• Finalise staff and helper duties for the event.
• Confirm the pool and travel arrangements.
• Prepare the recording of results.
• Organise first-aid.
• Check on all equipment needed.

On the day
• Prepare children to help set up and clear poolside.
• Take equipment needed to pool, eg aids, balls, hoops, whistles etc.
• Organise distribution of programmes, etc.

After the gala
• Awards or praise (as appropriate) to children who have participated.
• Thank all who have helped.
• Clear the pool of all clothes, litter and apparatus.
• Review the occasion with children and staff involved.
• Note ideas for possible future events.
• Display photos, drawings or other records of the event.

These suggestions can be adapted and developed to suit local circumstances. Whole-staff planning, with some involvement of the children, can help ensure a happy, active and successful gala, in which the skills learnt in swimming can have active expession.

Outdoor and adventurous activities

'I learn more outdoors – I think it's the oxygen, it's good for your brain'
(primary child discussing an outdoor trip)

Outdoor education can contribute to the development of the whole child, not only in acquiring skills and knowledge in a new setting, but also in promoting qualities of leadership, co-operation and ability to act as a member of a group in problem-solving situations. Outdoor pursuits can enrich children's experience and virtually all areas of the curriculum. They can be divided into adventurous activities which are part of PE and other outdoor cross-curricular activities. The principles of 'plan-do-review' are as important here as in other areas of PE. A programme of outdoor education can make a contribution to the intellectual as well as the personal and social development of the child – and can form the basis for life-long interests. This section provides a guide to the following:

- What to teach
- Planning outdoor activities.

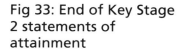

Fig 33: End of Key Stage 2 statements of attainment

The following diagram shows statements of attainment for PE which relate to outdoor and adventurous activities.

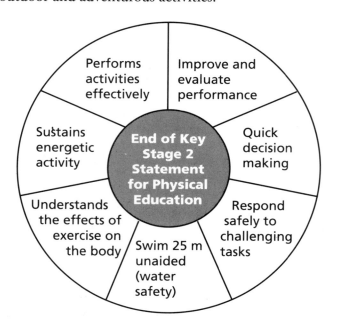

What to teach

The Programme of Study for outdoor and adventurous activities in the National Curriculum states that pupils should:

- be taught principles of safety in the outdoors and develop the ability to assess and respond to challenges in a variety of contexts and conditions;
- experience outdoor and adventurous activities in different environments (such as: school grounds and premises, parks, woodland and sea shore) that involve planning, navigation, working in small groups, recording and evaluating;
- be taught the skills necessary to the activity being undertaken with due regard to safety, including the correct use of appropriate equipment. *(PE in the National Curriculum)*

Such a programme should build on and extend what pupils have experienced as outdoor activities at Key Stage 1, such as short walks, places to climb, and scavenger hunts (looking for a number of items within a certain area). A programme of outdoor activities could be planned under the headings used in this section:

The school site
- Navigation: routes, maps, trail activities.
- Challenge: climbing/adventure apparatus, with opportunities for crawling, climbing, jumping, swinging and creative play.
- Fitness: vigorous activity on playground, keep-fit circuit or assault course in grounds.
- Campcraft: simple tent erection, rope craft, equipment, safety, country code/litter/conservation.

Local environments
(Parks, roads and rivers.)
- Navigation: routes, maps, bearings and compass work in local streets or village.
- Safety: Green Cross Code, (road, river, rail safety as appropriate).
- Challenge: learning activities linked with history, geography, RE, art, maths, science, etc.

Countryside environments
(Woodlands, country parks and hills.)
- Navigation: making/following routes, maps, and plans; compass work and orienteering tasks.
- Fitness: tracking, trails, rambles on different terrains; hill-walking leading to a mountain climb.
- Safety: negotiating streams, stiles, walls, marsh or bog; using country code, equipment, clothing, and mountain safety.
- Challenge: hill-walking, wide games in densely wooded areas; links with geography, nature trails and study.

Waterside environments

(Sea-shore, rivers, canals and reservoirs.)
- Navigation/challenge: treasure hunt, beachcombing, sea-shore or river trails.
- Fitness: towpath and coastal path walks, beach games and swimming.
- Safety: water safety codes, equipment, survival and life-saving skills.

Outdoor activity centres

(Residential centre, assault course or camping.)
- Navigation: with well-qualified staff and correct equipment.
- Challenge: new physical and problem-solving activities in an outdoor setting.
- Exploration: including canoeing, sailing, rock-climbing and abseiling, pony trekking, cycling, orienteering.
- Fitness: trails, walks, and vigorous physical activity.
- Safety: safety and first-aid in different outdoor environments, including the use of appropriate equipment.

Planning outdoor activities

In planning outdoor and adventurous activities, the 'plan-do-review' approach means involving the children as far as possible in organising and evaluating what you and they do.

Plan

Invite children to help plan outdoor activities either individually (by drawing up and sharing personal plans), through discussion in small groups (and then reporting back to the class) or as a whole-class discussion. A useful strategy is to share ideas in pairs or small groups first. Record ideas from each group to help in creating an information sheet to share with the class and to offer to parents.

Questions to ask in planning outdoor activities include: Where can we go? Where do we want to go? Why do we want to go? How will this visit help us (achieve our aims)? What can we do there? How long shall we go for? When shall we go? How shall we travel? What will the costs be? What clothing and equipment will be needed? How many helpers do we need? What do they need to be able to do? How shall we organise in groups? What rules shall we make? What do our parents need to know? What happens if something is lost or damaged, or someone is hurt? What do we need to know before we go? How can we find out? How will we record and share our experience? What will we do when we get back? Another strategy is to ask children to brainstorm the questions it would be useful to ask in planning an outdoor trip, and to list and share these for discussion. In this way, a whole visit can be planned and costed with the maximum involvement of the class.

Safety

Leaders of outdoor activities will need to ensure they follow the safety guidelines of the local education authority and and/or advice from the Department for Education (see *Safety in Outdoor Education* (HMSO, 1989)). Thorough preparation will involve a visit beforehand to the proposed location of the outdoor activity. Discuss aspects of safety with the children – what safety rules would they suggest?

Using the children's ideas, as well as published safety guidelines and information which may be available from the activity centre, you should be in a good position to check :

• The suitability of planned activities (and alternatives for special needs if required).
• Board and lodging arrangements (if appropriate).
• Pupil-teacher ratios for safety and supervision.
• Qualifications and experience of leaders or helpers.
• Equipment and clothing (suitability for weather and terrain).
• Health and travel insurance, legal liability, and insurance cover.
• Travel arrangements.
• Information for parents (via a meeting and information/consent forms).

Before the outdoor activity takes place, make sure all who need to be are aware of your plans, including the children, helpers, parents and school.

Do

During the outdoor activity will the children:
• Be active and involved?
• Be set challenging, but realistic and achievable goals?
• Be made aware of expectations/rules of good behaviour?
• Know and observe safety rules and country codes?
• Be suitably clothed and well resourced?
• Be supported and encouraged to try new skills and activities?
• Be given opportunities to lead, to follow and to work co-operatively?

Review

Taking time to reflect on experience is a valuable part of learning. This review might be part of a class-based language or topic lesson in a relevant subject area, or be part of a PE session in the classroom.

Tasks can include:

• Writing and describing their activities (diary, creative prose or poetry worksheet, or in answer to questions).
• Writing and describing a specific activity for others to follow, with diagrams and pictures.

- Writing articles for class or school magazine, PTA or governors' newsletters, or a local newspaper.
- Sending letters (or audio tapes) of thanks to those who have helped at the activity centre.
- Discussing and reviewing the activities, organisation, and learning outcomes of the visit.
- Recording advice, or answering a questionnaire for a future class who may make a similar visit.
- Preparing a presentation to 'show and tell' at a school assembly.
- Creating a display of visual (drawings, art/craftwork, photos, video) and written material about the trip.

It is useful to keep a record and information about a major outdoor experience with your class in a resource file for future reference. This may help others in their planning, and to answer those perennial questions: What outdoor activities shall I plan for this class? Where shall we go? What shall we do?

The following are some suggested activities that children could experience in differing environments as part of a programme for outdoor and adventurous activity in the primary school.

The school site

Navigation activities

Warm-up games and challenges
- On signal, run to various parts of the area (eg walls, lines, shapes, colours, items beginning with ...).
- North, South, East and West: skip, run or jump to a distant compass point on a given signal. How long before all the class arrive (extend to perform an exercise on arrival)?
- Traffic lights stop, ready, go, according to visual or oral colour commands.
- Follow the lines or markings on the playground; keep changing direction – no touching.
- Litter chase: pick up as many pieces of litter as possible in a set time (wash hands at the end of the lesson).
- Exercise trail (with playground or site signs by each exercise point clearly numbered): Children in groups of 2 or 3 can rotate in sequence, or complete in random order. Children undertake an exercise task at each point of the given trail, and move on at a signal.

Card games

Distribute matched cards (matching pairs) amongst the children to play:

- **Snap:** find a partner with a matching card (letter, number, sign, apparatus picture). Together, find the object in the hall or play area and return to teacher. Take a new card.

(a)

Vicar = Church

Reverse

Jog = 20

- **Pairs:** distribute paired cards amongst the class. Find your partner with a paired card; (examples of paired cards: 2x6/12; vicar/church; London/Thames; St Patrick/Ireland, etc, according to topic). On the back of one card will be an activity, on the other a number. The pair perform the activity that number of times. Return to teacher, take a new card (a).

- **Conewords:** Stick or place 12 or more paired names under cones scattered in area (there should be many more cones without names). Individually or in pairs, children search and write down all the names on a sheet and then match them according to topic (eg VI/6; la maison/house; William Shakespeare, etc).

- **Anagram:** children search for cards in twos and threes, having been directed with a strong clue to a different card in the area (under bench, near sandpit, etc). On the card is a letter; on the reverse, a sign or clue for the position of the next card (eg East 30 paces, under log). Each card contains one letter of the anagram, and the unscrambled letters make a topic word.

- **Trails:** i) make up a trail for another pair to follow: a)written; b) on audio tape; ii) follow a broken trail of sand, paper, or cubes. Collect information or solve problems en route (eg anagram letters/words/number problem); iii) blind trail: guide a partner, blindfolded, through obstacles in the hall or playground: a) touching; b) with oral instructions only; iv) scavenger trail: find articles hidden in area; record on card or remember what is found: a) search at random; b) search in set order (with the clue for the next article given on the object or card). Compass points/bearings can be introduced when appropriate.

Challenge and fitness activities

Obstacle course

Use hall or adventure apparatus to set tasks for pairs or groups to:

- Travel around/over/under the apparatus without touching the floor.
- Travel as above, but in contact with each other.
- Plan a route or task for another pair to follow.

Map swap

Each pair designs a simple map of class/hall/playground/site with symbols for easy route finding. Exchange maps to see how many features can be found (in correct order in a set time).

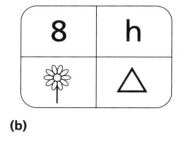

(b)

Card trail (shape)

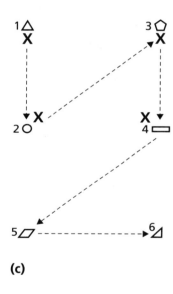

1 By Sandpit △
2 South 20m ○
3 N. West 30m ⬠
4 South 20m ▭
5 S. West 30m ▱
6 East 25m ◹

(c)

Orienteering

Place multi-symbol laminated signs throughout the grounds (on trees, walls, fences, etc) (b). Provide four differentiated clues to suit the group's ability (eg, letters, numbers, symbols, shapes). Trails can be numbers only, symbols only, or a combination of signs for variety. Distribute cards to each pair; these can be verbal clues, or compass points and paces, or bearings and paces, to use with a map of the grounds. Variety can be achieved by changing the order in which the signs are found by each group (c). **Note:** make the location of the first card easy for each pair or group.

Navigation and safety activities
Flag search

In pairs or groups, design a route in the school grounds or the immediate environment outside school (preferably without crossing major roads and with plenty of parent supervision and help). Groups will have to:

- Make flags (one colour per group) with a letter or number on the reverse, at marker points around the route.
- Draw flags on a route map (the group can draw a map or one can be prepared).
- Draw symbols of road features on the map (eg PB for post box, T for telephone, H for hydrant, + for church, Z for zebra, P for pelican crossing, etc).
- Include a key for symbols.
- Reverse letters can be an anagram of a suitable linked topic, or numbers could add up to a target number.

Green Cross Code

With adequate supervision and instruction, road safety procedures and questions can be included as part of the route. Maybe your local policeman could help!

Adventurous and problem-solving activities
Tanks

Groups of four to six children with two mats. Standing on one mat, children lift the second mat above their heads and then lay it down in a new place, so that all the children are able to move on to it without touching the ground. Keep repeating a) as far as possible in a set time; b) around a course. If the floor is touched start again, or go back five metres, or deduct time faults.

Log jam

In groups of five to ten children stand on a log or bench. Without touching the floor, they order themselves from end to end according to size/age/height, etc. Can they think of other ways of ordering themselves?

Chained

In pairs or small groups, children negotiate apparatus or course while joined (hands held, arms interlocked, ankles tied).

Sardines

With the children in groups of six to twelve, arrange small/large hoops, low, flat surfaces or chalked shapes in the area. How many can stand in or on the apparatus at one time: a)using both feet; b) on one foot; c) sitting; d) lying down; e) any other ways?

Blind

Groups of four to six. One calls out instructions: 'Forward five, right three', etc, or calls compass points or bearings, for blindfolded members of the group to negotiate the course, or for others in the group to carry a mat or bench.

Rescue

Groups of four to six travel over the apparatus or around a small course while carrying an injured person (a mat or a plank).

Commando

Groups travel around the apparatus, or the adventure playground course, helping each other across or over difficult places (eg over bars, swinging on ropes, jumping across a gap). The group is timed when all are 'home'.

Adventurous activities in the playground or school grounds

The following ideas for vigorous and adventurous activity can be adapted to suit the age and ability of your pupils. Children can also be given the opportunities to create challenges for each other, related to each activity. Personal best achievement can be recorded, and children encouraged to set themselves realistic goals.

- Each child shuttle runs for one minute between two posts or trees eight to ten metres apart.
- How many step-ups on a log, bench or seat can be achieved in 30 seconds?
- Travel along a suspended rope, bar or ladder: how long does it take?
- Travel over/under/around pieces of adventure apparatus without touching the ground.
- Negotiate different pieces of apparatus, over or under, in a short, circular route.
- Get over or under a suspended bar/bench/pole in any way you can.
- Get on (to stand with a stretch) and off (to touch the ground with hands) an object or piece of apparatus as often as possible in a set time.
- Jump to reach a marker (chalk mark on wall or tree, 20–30 cm or more above the child's stretch height).

- Balance and walk across a narrow log, pole or upturned bench: forwards, backwards, and sideways.
- Swing on a rope across one log, mat or bench, to another.
- Climb up a ladder/rope/net/bars; climb down until ready to jump to a safe landing. Repeat for 30 – 60 seconds.
- Crawl through vertical or suspended hoops and tyres.
- Crawl through or under scrambling net or large barrels.
- Traverse (sideways, using hands and feet) a low wall, ledge or rope bridge.

Other examples of outdoor and adventurous activities in the school environment include use of climbing apparatus (see below). For further ideas for gymnastic activities see p26, especially the themes on travel and use of space, supporting body weight, and the section on large apparatus. For warm-up ideas use any of the activities and games in the Games or Athletics sections (pp76, 104). Children can work in groups on different outdoor activities; for example, other skills or tasks can include knots, campcraft, measuring, mapping or other orienteering skills.

List other activities that you and the children can think of, which are suited to your school environment.

Outdoor climbing frame

The following are some activities for use on an outdoor climbing frame:

- Get on and off in different ways – how many ways?
- Find different places to get on and off – how many places?
- Travel over, under, through and round apparatus without touching anyone – how many routes?
- Find different places to support yourself on hands and feet only on the apparatus.
- Find other body parts which will support your weight on the apparatus – which parts?
- Hang, using hands only or backs of knees – how many ways to hang?
- Balance on the apparatus on hands and feet/tummy/bottom.
- Find different ways to be upside down on the apparatus.
- Move from a hanging or balance position on a low level, to one as high as you can.
- Balance or hang to make curled/stretched/twisted shapes.
- Join together three different hanging and balance shapes.
- Find places to climb up and down, slide, crawl, jump, drop down, or swing.
- Find places to twist, turn and rotate your body.
- Link together a hang, swing and a jump with a deep controlled landing.
- Link together any three movements of your own choice.

Outdoor climbing or adventure apparatus has the potential for these and other activities and experiences, such as creative and dramatic play:

the apparatus can be used as a fort, a spacecraft, another planet, Noah's Ark, a ship, an island, a mountain, a block of flats, a tree, etc, and can be used as a link with drama, RE, English and in any cross-curricular topic.

Local environment

Your local environment may provide opportunities for outdoor and adventurous activities, such as walking, jogging, climbing, adventurous play, tracking, other orientation skills or campcraft. The following are some suggestions for activities in local environments, such as parks or other public places:

Fun running

Group or class jogging and walking around a local course, eg walk 100 paces, then run 100 paces alternately. Extend the activity by providing children with challenges, such as traversing obstacles (streams, logs, or tree trunks), rolling down hills, and under obstacles. Make it fun, not competitive, aiming for the whole group or class to make a sustained effort.

Training runs

• How far around a course or circuit can individuals run in in a set time without stopping?
• How long does it take individuals to complete a training circuit, running or jogging?
Personal best performances are the individual goals.

Park trail

Display 10 – 20 natural items to the class (eg grass, a buttercup, leaves, twigs, cones, feathers, a conker, a chestnut). In pairs, children must memorise, then collect as many items as possible in a set time. They may return, together, for a prompt to aid memory, but this will slow them down. How many items can they find in a set time?

Hare and hounds

Divide children into a few hares and many hounds. Each hare is to be chased by a pack of four or five hounds. Hares run off with a collection of items to drop, eg pieces of paper, conkers, etc. Hounds follow hares (after about five minutes) searching for and picking up as many items as possible dropped by hares around the course or circuit.

Arrow trails

Like hares and hounds except hares leave arrow signs where they run. Decoy trails can be laid for hounds, who hunt in packs of four or five. Hares try to return to the start before they are captured (touched) by the hounds.

Wide games (in a wooded area)
- **Search:** class to search for six children (hares) hiding in the bushes or trees. Either the class has to find them in a set time, or the hares must get to a warren (the home base) without being caught.
- **Flags:** class is divided into team A (about 10 children) and team B (about 20 children). Team A go and hide five to ten flags (or other items) behind trees, bushes, etc in a defined area. On signal, team B search, to try to find the flags. They must try to return to base with the flags they find without being touched by a member of team A.
- **Fox and rabbits:** rabbits, all with braids as tails tucked into their shorts, go into hiding. The foxes search for them. On detection, the rabbits make for 'ground' (the home base) before their tails are taken by a fox. (The rabbits may keep changing their hiding places.)
- **Commandos:** the teacher protects a large HQ (at least 5x5 m). The children, 50 m away in a heavily wooded area, crawl as near to the HQ as possible (or even into it) before the teacher can identify the commandos by name and location. If spotted, identified and named by the teacher, commandos retreat back to the 50m mark and try again.

Note: commandos can dirty their faces, put ferns into their headgear and clothing, etc as camouflage.

Countryside environments

Walks and nature trails can involve a cross-curricular approach: biological, geographical, aesthetic and physical. Children can undertake navigation activities, improve their fitness and learn to understand and appreciate a countryside environment. Preparation for a countryside outing may involve:
- Study of flora and fauna of the area.
- Route-finding, mapping (eg studying Ordnance Survey (OS) maps), compass skills.
- Local history and geography of area.
- Safety procedures and boundaries.

Activities during the walk could include:
- Being blindfolded and led by a partner.
- Touching trees/barks and other textures.
- Walking on or through different terrains.
- Touching/smelling small trees, flowers, herbs, shrubs, etc.
- Photographing/sketching special items of interest.
- Listening for sounds/calls/song by a pond, river or woodland.
- Studying key features and recording them on a map or chart.
- Playing an active game (see above).

At the end of the trail, or from an appropriate point, the children can find their way back to the start in pairs or groups using map/compass/bearings as appropriate. Follow-up activities could include:

- Drawing, painting and mounting their observations.
- Mapping the trail and details of route features.
- Diary or questionnaire of walk.
- Observation and evaluation of the activities.
- Explaining their trail, with the help of a large OS map, to another class.

Hill-walking

Many of the suggestions for country and nature trails also apply to hill-walking, but these additional points should be particularly stressed.

Preparation
- Correct clothing and footwear (waterproofs and boots).
- Country and mountain codes for safety and conservation.
- Map, compass and route-finding.
- One teacher/instructor should have mountain leadership certificate.

Suggestions to start
- Choose a simple route, adventurous but not too long.
- Include one climb or descent.
- Choose a walk with lots of focus and interest points (stiles, fences, gates, streams, rocks, trees, wildlife, farmstock, stepping-stones, marshland).

During the walk
- Keep a slow, steady and rhythmical pace.
- One leader per group of eight approximately (three to four per class), or two for a group of 16; one at the front and one at the back.
- Rotate the children as walk leaders.
- Walk at the pace of the slowest child.
- Maintain interest and motivation with reference points of observation, short-term objectives, or challenges and responsibilities for the children.

Waterside environments

Primary children should have experience of both sea and freshwater environments. A trip to the seaside offers many learning opportunities, as does a towpath walk.

Seaside trip
Activities by the sea, on the beach, among the rocks and on cliff tops provide a rich variety of cross-curricular work involving geography, biology and physical education. Children can improve navigational

skills, take part in new physical activities in and out of the sea, study rocks, minerals and marine life, and enjoy the aesthetic and sensory pleasures that such a visit can bring. Preparation for such a visit might include:

- Study of rocks, minerals and sea life.
- Water safety, and the work of coastguards.
- Study of tides and currents.
- Planning the route, journey, costs and timetables.
  See 'plan, do, review' ideas (pp154–155).

Activities at the seaside
- Treasure/scavenger hunt for pebbles, shells, seaweeds, etc.
- Beachcombing for flotsam and jetsam and investigation of its source; pollution; etc.
- Sketching, photography or birdwatching.
- Fishing or crabbing.
- A pre-lunch swim or paddle in designated areas (observing safety flags) with adults marking the limit of the bathing area.
- Tag, ball or frisbee games in the shallows or sand pools.
- Beach games of soft ball, cricket, rounders, rugby touch.
- Beach games, relays, and small apparatus games of 2v2, 3v3.
- Sand, shell and pebble castles or model-making.
- Coastal walk trail: see nature trail activities (p162).

Follow-up activities
Follow-up activities could include those similar to the nature trail; other activities might include drawing a map/plan of the route; diagrams and maps of the coastline; beach/water safety posters; photographs/pictures to study; pollution/conservation investigation; and an exhibition of work.

Freshwater towpath walk
Many schools are located near canals or rivers, which make ideal nature rambles or walks, linking with topics such as water, rivers, bridges, water transport, canals and locks. There may be the possibility of liaising with a local yacht or canoe club for water sports, such as sailing and canoeing, with expert tuition in suitable, safe water conditions. Alternatively, a motor boat or steamer journey could be made in one direction with a towpath walk in the other.

Areas of study
- Flora and fauna en route.
- River/canal transport.
- Leisure pursuits.
- Water birds/habitats/nesting.

- Tides and currents.
- Locks and waterside information.
- Water safety and rescue.
- Conservation/pollution/water treatment.
- Water craft, boatbuilding and design.

Physical activities
- Towpath walk or nature trail.
- Jogging or walking along towpaths.
- Cycling.
- Fishing.
- Canoeing or sailing (if there is a canoe club nearby, there may be an opportunity for practice in a local river, lake or swimming pool for confidence and capsize skills).

Outdoor activity centres

One of the most exciting experiences for youngsters is a weekend (or longer) spent at a residential centre with qualified instructors for activities such as canoeing, sailing, rock-climbing, caving, pony trekking, etc. Opportunities for personal and social education are immense, with children becoming more self-aware, and building confidence and trust in each other and their teachers. The experience of leaving home, perhaps for the first time, and sharing 'house' with others in a secure environment can be valuable in developing maturity and self-confidence.

For preparations and planning for such a school visit see 'plan-do-review' (pp154–155). Ensure that the centre to be visited is a bona fide centre with experienced instruction and equipment. It is essential to have visited the centre and sampled the activities yourself.

Children are often divided into groups of ten for adventurous activities, and it is advisable to have a teacher, as well as the instructor, with each group. This will allow you to support, encourage and motivate individuals when necessary. Encourage the centre to allow children to do some of the chores: helping at meal times, cleaning up, and preparing equipment.

Awards for caring, sharing, helpfulness, improvement, sense of humour, and courage, can be awarded daily or at the end of the stay. Try to link environmental study with adventurous activities for a well-balanced week. Ensure there is time to relax and enjoy talking and sharing experiences; this could happen before bedtime, when reflection, prayer and singing can round off the day in the best possible way.

In planning, ensure all help keep to the rules of the centre, and are involved in making sensible rules for bedtimes, sleeping, eating, refreshments, room arrangements, safety, emergencies, first-aid and health.

Camping

Perhaps you can create your own outdoor activity centre by camping in the school grounds, or at an alternative venue. This would provide an ideal opportunity to learn campcraft skills, which could include:

- Tent selection/types.
- Tent erection/striking/packing.
- Site planning/organising a camp weekend.
- Kit preparation/packing/kit inspection.
- Simple ropework/knots/lashings.
- Camp rules and safety.
- Simple cooking/meal preparation (invitations to meal?).
- Link with tracking, route-planning skills and wide games (see pp156–162).

Canoeing

Canadian canoeing with a crew of three or four, including a teacher, is especially useful and enjoyable for beginners. Slalom and kayak canoes are great fun, but many junior children find them hard to control in windy conditions. Double kayaks for a timid child + teacher can prove helpful, or kayaks lashed together for more stability can help confidence and enjoyment. Is there a local club near you with coaches who can help?

Caving

This adventurous activity requires special preparation and equipment, but there may be members of caving clubs keen to help. Caving provides an opportunity for unique experiences, develops teamwork and patience through physical activity, and provides some insight into geology and other sciences.

Skiing

Expensive unless there is an artificial slope nearby. It can be related to study in science, geography and history. While enormous fun and a great challenge in balance and co-ordination it is best left for later experience at secondary school.

Activities such as these, if they are fun, well-organised and satisfying experiences, can form the basis of more advanced outdoor activities and leisure pursuits in later life.

For Resources for outdoor and adventurous activity see p190.
For Assessment of outdoor and adventurous activity see pp169, 174.

Assessing and recording achievement

'Assessment of pupils' attainment is a continous process and is integral to all teaching and learning. It will inform teachers and pupils (and parents) about progress, and help to identify learner strengths, weaknesses and needs.'
(Non-Statutory Guidance in PE, 1992)

Your day-to-day observations in the PE lesson will tell you much about your children's physical achievements and capabilities. Some of these assessments will need to be recorded, for 'teachers will need to refer to their own continuous assessment during the key stage to report on a pupil's achievement at the end of the key stage.'
(Non-Statutory Guidance, 1992).

The principles that should govern record-keeping in PE can be summed up as:

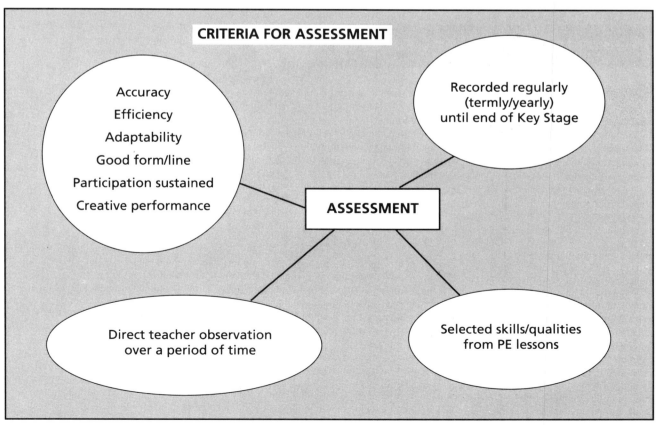

CRITERIA FOR ASSESSMENT

Accuracy
Efficiency
Adaptability
Good form/line
Participation sustained
Creative performance

Recorded regularly
(termly/yearly)
until end of Key Stage

ASSESSMENT

Direct teacher observation
over a period of time

Selected skills/qualities
from PE lessons

The following record sheets are designed to make your task easier by offering ways of recording only the key elements of progress that occur within the normal PE programme. Progress can be recorded termly, yearly or at the end of the key stage. They are photocopiable, and you may wish to add to or amend them to suit your own needs. Use whatever recording method suits you. The two following methods are simple and allow for recording of progression:

a) / = experience of activity   ✓ = competent/confident
or
b) / = below average   ∠ = average ability
   △ = above average   ▲ = excellent

The record sheets include space for comment on such areas as growth, attitude, maturity and special needs. They also include teacher assessment records for individual children in the key areas of PE and class records of achievements and experiences in PE. These records include opportunities to make a qualitative assessment and to make particular comments on successes or difficulties encountered. There are also sample record sheets for self-assessment in PE for the children in your class. These are photo-copiable, and may be adapted or developed to suit your needs.
(Note: The self-assessment sheets are adapted from *Recording Achievement in Primary Schools* by R Fisher. Published by Simon & Schuster, 1991)

Teacher assessment records

Class records

Gymnastics
The suggested skills and qualities to be observed in gymnastics are:
• Flexibility: bending, stretching, twisting and extending the body.
• Agility: spring, speed and lightness.
• Body control: balance, landing, posture and poise.
• Creativity: exploration and inventiveness.

Dance
The suggested skills and qualities to be observed in dance are:
• Body actions: dance movements and patterns.
• Form: body line, control and posture.
• Expressive quality: sensitivity to mood and stimuli.
• Creativity: exploration and invention of movement ideas.

Games

The suggested skills and qualities to be observed in games are:
- Ball skills (hand/eye): catching, throwing, passing.
- Ball footskills: dribbling, kicking, ball control,
- Striking: co-ordination, accuracy.
- Invasion games: understanding attack and defence.
- Net and wall games: accuracy, anticipation, reaction.
- Inventiveness: exploring and creating new ideas for games activity.

Athletics

The suggested skills and qualities to be observed in athletics are:
- Running: sprinting, keeping straight line, co-ordination.
- Jumping: spring, lift, landing.
- Throwing (small ball): overarm, sideways body action.
- Fitness: endurance, sustained running.

Outdoor activities

The suggested skills and qualities to be observed in outdoor activities are:
- Navigation: mapping, compass-reading, tracking.
- Activities: indicate outdoor activities and experiences.
- Safety codes: understanding safety in water and land environments.
- Country code: understanding of conservation and pollution; care of the countryside.

Swimming

The suggested skills and qualities to be observed in swimming are:
- Swimming: eg 10, 25, 50 metres unaided (state distance achieved).
- Diving: crouch, standing, plunge dives.
- Personal survival: floating, treading water, underwater swimming.
- Strokes: indicate swimming strokes in which competency is shown.

General qualities in PE

General qualities to be assessed in all areas of PE include:
- Observing rules: eg of games, referees, safety, behaviour.
- Sporting attitudes: fairness, commitment, acceptance of victory or defeat.
- Co-operation: works well in a team, supportive, helps others.
- Leadership: can lead others, shows good example.
- Decision-making: able to make quick decisions, thoughtful responses.
- Planning: able to think ahead, to discuss ideas and plans.
- Practising: sustains activity, seeks to improve performance.
- Reviewing: able to recognise, describe and evaluate outcomes of activity.

Note: you may wish to amend these skills and qualities according to your circumstances. If you are unable to assess each item, then your comments can highlight special abilities or needs.

RECORD OF ACHIEVEMENT – GYMNASTICS

CLASS/YEAR...

	Names	Flexibility	Agility	Body control	Creativity	Comments
1						
2						
3						
4						
5						
6						
7						
8						
9						
10						
11						
12						
13						
14						
15						
16						
17						
18						
19						
20						
21						
22						
23						
24						
25						
26						
27						
28						
29						
30						

RECORD OF ACHIEVEMENT – DANCE

CLASS/YEAR...

	Names	Body actions	Form	Expressive quality	Creative movement	Comments
1						
2						
3						
4						
5						
6						
7						
8						
9						
10						
11						
12						
13						
14						
15						
16						
17						
18						
19						
20						
21						
22						
23						
24						
25						
26						
27						
28						
29						
30						

 **RECORD OF ACHIEVEMENT – Games and Athletics**

CLASS/YEAR...

	Names	Running	Jumping	Throwing (small ball)	Ball skills (large ball)	Striking	Inventiveness	Comments
1								
2								
3								
4								
5								
6								
7								
8								
9								
10								
11								
12								
13								
14								
15								
16								
17								
18								
19								
20								
21								
22								
23								
24								
25								
26								
27								
28								
29								
30								

RECORD OF ACHIEVEMENT – Outdoor and adventurous activities

NAME..

Activities	Y3	Y4	Y5	Y6	Comments

RECORD OF ACHIEVEMENT – Swimming

CLASS/YEAR...

	Names	Water confidence	Move under water	Front (with aids)	Back (Iwith aids)	10/25m (front)	10/25m (back)	Comments
I								
2								
3								
4								
5								
6								
7								
8								
9								
10								
11								
12								
13								
14								
15								
16								
17								
18								
19								
20								
21								
22								
23								
24								
25								
26								
27								
28								
29								
30								

RECORD OF ACHIEVEMENT – Physical education

NAME.. DATE........................

End of key stage statements for Key Stage 2:

Pupils should be able to:

a) plan, practise, improve and remember more complex sequences of movement;

b) Perform effectively in activities requiring quick decision making;

c) respond safely, alone and with others, to challenging tasks, taking account of levels of skill and understanding;

d) swim unaided for at least 25 metres and demonstrate an understanding of water safety;

e) evaluate how well they and others perform and behave against criteria suggested by the teacher, and suggest ways of improving performance;

f) sustain energetic activity over appropriate periods of time in a range of physical activities and understand the effects of exercise on the body.

Examples of progress/achievement

General comments

Teacher...

Self-assessment records (by the child)

My achievements in PE

This record sheet invites the child to record areas of success in PE, eg new skills, games played, times and distances achieved, etc.

Achievements and experiences in PE

This record sheet invites the child to reflect on a PE experience, or series of experiences, and to record, describe and evaluate the experience. (Children who have difficulties in writing can have their words scribed by a teacher or helper.)

My record of achievement in PE

This record sheet invites the child to write a report based on a series of questions about PE, for an annual, half-yearly or termly report on PE. (An alternative approach would be to ask children to suggest questions or categories for such a report.)

My report of the the year

This record sheet offers children the opportunity to write and/or draw what they have done, enjoyed and achieved in their year of PE lessons. (Discuss or display the different elements of the PE programme they may wish to comment on: gymnastics, dance, games, athletics, outdoor activities and swimming.)

WHAT I CAN DO IN PE

Name...Date of birth.............

Achievement	Date

WHAT I DID IN PE

    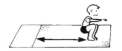

Name...Date...............

What I did

What was good about it?

My record of achievement in PE

Name...School year...................

My school................................My teacher...................

What I can do in PE

The best things about me in PE

What I like in PE

What games I play

How I have improved this year

What I want to do next year

Signed..Date............................

My report of the year in PE

    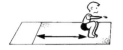

Name..Year...............

Special needs

Teachers need to be very aware of all kinds of physical disability that may present themselves in the mainstream school, from the very timid or poorly co-ordinated child, to the child with a specific physical limitation.

Most children with a physical disability need more exercise than National Curriculum requirements. They should take part in all activities alongside other children where possible, so that they adapt naturally and use their bodies in the most effective way. It may be that a Statement of Special Educational Needs will have been made before the child enters primary school, and additional classroom support may be available. However, there will be some children with such a statement who do not have special needs in PE, and many children with special needs in PE who are seen to be making satisfactory progress in all other areas of the curriculum. There are also some children who are specially gifted at PE, or at aspects of PE, who will, at some time in their school career, need special coaching in out-of-school clubs if their talents are to be fully realised.

The experimental and challenging approaches that are part of good practice in PE are particularly suited to children with different needs and abilities, although some special provision for children with special needs may have to be made. The suggestions below may prove helpful.

Physically disabled
- Let them practise the skills already learned/the abilities they have.
- Look for planning/leadership/evaluative skills – not just performance.
- Encourage mobility exercises advised by physiotherapist.
- Adapt apparatus and explore new ideas to suit needs (other children can be encouraged to plan this).
- Considerations: size and weight of balls; size, weight and width of bats; height of benches, tables, targets; distance of target, partner; wheelchair activities/non-wheelchair activities.

Hearing-impaired children
- Face the children, reduce background noise and speak slowly and clearly.
- Agree a touch signal that all can use for 'stop' or 'watch'.
- Demonstrate activity when appropriate.
- Move with child/hold hand where necessary.
- Encourage use of vibration/rhythm experiences in movement.

Visually impaired children

- Agree a stop signal for all to use; use a child's name before speaking.
- If possible provide brightly coloured/shiny/crinkly apparatus that can be picked out, felt and heard when used.
- Use small equipment with bright colours and different textures.
- Encourage children to listen and feel their way to apparatus.
- Use partner Buddy system where appropriate.
- Encourage running in free, open spaces at first.

Moderate learning difficulties/poor motor co-ordination

- Clear, simple instructions; lots of praise and motivation.
- Set clear achievement targets; expect them to be achieved in easy stages.
- Active adult support in gross and locomotor activities. Severe cases should be referred for statement/physiotherapist help.
- Use adapted equipment where necessary.

Asthma sufferers are encouraged to take medication and exercise in order to combat an attack. Advice from parents and doctor is essential.

Diabetes sufferers can take part in all activities, but staff must be aware of child's eating pattern/insulin reaction. Watch for signs of breathlessness, dizziness or discomfort.

Epileptics are encouraged to take part in PE activities, but there may be risk situations to avoid, or in which a partner should be employed. (Special care should be taken when swimming or during adventurous activities. Medical advice should be sought beforehand.)

Resources for PE

The following are some suggested resources for PE with juniors:

Indoor area – the school hall

In most schools, the hall will be a multi-purpose area for lunch, assembly, music and drama as well as for PE activities. Ensure that it is safe for physical activity. Check for any wet or slippery patches, especially after lunch, and that any furniture does not project dangerously into the teaching area.

Large apparatus for PE is best spaced round the sides of the hall for ease of access; labels on the walls will help to remind everyone of its position. Small apparatus and games equipment can be stored in a wide cupbopard. It may also be possible to have a secure shed or outbuilding near the playground or field for games equipment.

Outdoor areas

The playground

Check regularly that the play surface is safe and free from potential dangers such as loose gravel, glass or animal waste (for further information see Playground Safety Guidelines available from DE, Sanctuary Buildings, Great Smith St, London SW1 3BT).

Playgrounds can be made stimulating areas for both imaginative and recreational play. See Outdoor and adventurous activities (pp156, 184, 188).

Markings

The following markings on the play area can be used during PE sessions, when appropriate, and can encourage children to practice lesson activities during playtimes. It is not intended that all these markings be included on one playground. Turn the design of playground markings into a learning opportunity by discussing possible designs with children. Ask older children to draw their own markings for playground games. Try to involve children in the decisions you or colleagues make about playground markings and play apparatus.

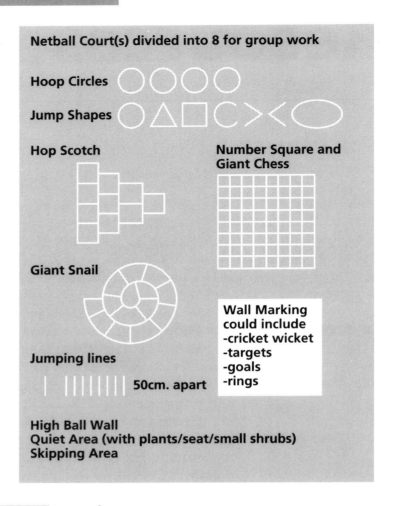

Fig 34: Some playground markings for PE

Netball Court(s) divided into 8 for group work

Hoop Circles

Jump Shapes

Hop Scotch

Number Square and Giant Chess

Giant Snail

Wall Marking could include
-cricket wicket
-targets
-goals
-rings

Jumping lines

50cm. apart

High Ball Wall
Quiet Area (with plants/seat/small shrubs)
Skipping Area

Gymnastics

Apparatus

Gymnastic apparatus should, where possible, be light, adjustable, and of good quality. When stored, it should be easily accessible, and checked regularly for safety. The following is a list of basic gymnastic apparatus:

- fixed or foldaway climbing frame, bars and ropes;
- round or hexagonal agility table;
- stacking, rectangular agility tables;
- ladder, trestle trees, low balance beam, wooden or padded planks;
- padded stools;
- balance benches;
- twelve agility mats (in four colours);
- safety landing mat (for JM/I schools);
- mat trolleys can be useful for transporting mats, but can be troublesome if quick access/storage is required. Other possibilities include small mats (approximately 100x60 cm), hexagonal mats, or an adjustable bar box.

Further reading

BAALPE (1990), *Safe Practice in PE*
Buckland, D (1970), *Gymnastics* (Heinemann)
Carroll, H and Manners, H (1992), *Gymnastics 7–11* (Falmer Press)
Jackman, J and Currier, B (1992), *Gymnastic Skills and Games* (Black)
Williams, A (1987), *Curriculum Gymnastics* (Hodder & Stoughton)
Wetton, P (1992), *Practical Guides: Physical Education* (Scholastic)

Useful addresses

- PE Association, Ling House, Unit 5, Western Court, Bromley Street, Birmingham B94 4AN
- Health Education Council, Hamilton House, Mabledon Place, London WC1H 9TX
- British Heart Foundation Jump Rope Scheme, Dept of PE & Sports Studies, Loughborough University, Loughborough, Leicestershire LE11 3TU

Dance

Equipment

Dance equipment could include:
- a robust, good quality record/cassette player or midi system;
- a small cassette player for flexible class use;
- a variety of tuned and untuned percussion instruments, eg tambourine, drum, triangle, chime bars, castanets, coconut shells, cymbals, maracas, shakers and children's class-made instruments.

Music

- a range of tapes, CDs or discs for dance, including examples from pop, rock, soul, jazz, TV themes, BBC sound effects, and collections of music from many cultures. Suggestions for classical music suitable for dance include:

Arnold: *English and Scottish Dances*
Bach: *Air on a G string*
Bernstein: *West Side Story*
Bizet: *Jeux D'Enfants*
Borodin: *Polovtsian Dances*
Chopin: *Minute Waltz*
Copland: *Appalachian Spring (canon on Lord of the Dance), Rodeo/Billy the Kid*
Debussy: *The Children's Corner Suite*
Dukas: *The Sorcerer's Apprentice*
da Falla: *Ritual Fire Dance* (from *El Amo Brujo*)
Glass: *Powaqqatsi*
Grieg: *Peer Gynt Suite (In the Hall of the Mountain King)*
Handel: *Arrival of the Queen of Sheba*
Herold: *La Fille mal Gardée (Clog Dance)*
Holst: *The Planets Suite*
Ibert: *Circus/Invitation to Dance*

Jean Michel Jarre: *selections*
Scott Joplin: *The Sting, Elite Syncopations*
Rimsky Korsakov: *Cappriccio Espagnol, Flight of the Bumble Bee*
John Lanchbery: *Tales of Beatrix Potter*
Mozart: *March no 1 in D*
Mussorgsky: *Night on a Bare Mountain, Pictures at an Exhibition*
Prokofiev: *Peter & the Wolf, Romeo & Juliet*
Ravel: *Bolero*
Saint-Saens: *Carnival of the Animals*
Sousa: marches, eg *Stars and Stripes Forever*
Tchaikovsky: *Nutcracker Suite*
Strauss: *Radetsky March*
Vivaldi: *Four Seasons*
Warlock: *Capriol Suite*
Vaughan Williams: *Fantasia on Greensleeves*

Poetry sources for dance

Poetry books with suitable poems as a stimulus for dance include:

Baldwin and Whitehead, 1972, *That way and This:Poetry for Creative Dance* (Chatto & Windus)

Fisher, R (ed) anthologies: *Amazing Monsters, Funny Folk, Ghosts Galore, Witch Words, Pet poems, Minibeasts* (Faber and Faber)

Rosen, M (ed), 1991, *The Kingfisher Book of Children's Poetry* (Kingfisher Books)

Slater, 1990, *A Ring o' Roses: Poems for Movement and Dance* (Northcote House)

Further reading on dance

Arts Council: *Dance in Schools* (Arts Council Guidance on Dance Education, 1993)

BBC: *Let's Dance* – a handbook for teachers by Mary Harlow and Linda Rolfe

BBC: *Look! Look what I can do!* by Kate Harrison

Violet Bruce: *Movement and Dance in the Primary School* (Open University Press, 1988)

Harrison, K *Bright Ideas: Dance and Movement* (Scholastic)

Mary Lowden: *Dancing to Learn* (Falmer Press, 1989)

Joan Russell: *Creative Dance in the Primary School* (Northcote House, 1992)

Rosamund Shreeves: *Children Dancing* (Ward Lock, 1990)

Useful addresses for dance

English Folk Dance and Song Society, Cecil Sharp House, 2 Regents Park Road, London NW1 7AY

Primrose Education Resources, White Cross, Lancaster LA1 4DQ

Coomber Electronic Equipment, Croft Walk, Worcester WR1 3NZ

Games

The following is a list of basic games equipment for juniors:

- first-aid case;
- 40 bean bags (in four colours);
- 40 medium plastic balls, 10–14 cm diameter, light and brightly coloured;
- 20 large plastic practice footballs plus six match footballs (size 4);
- 6 match netballs (size 4);
- 20 plastic rugby balls plus 10 'softy' practice rugby balls plus 6 match rugby balls (size 4);
- 20 airflo or small foam balls;
- 40 tennis or rubber balls;
- 30 small wooden bats (for tennis);

- 2 sets of short tennis bats and equipment;
- 6 each of rounders, cricket and hockey balls;
- 30 flat rounders bats plus 6 rounders bats;
- 30 cricket bat shapes plus 6 cricket bats (sizes 3 and 4) plus a set of playground stumps and cricket equipment (in bag);
- 30 mini hockey or shinty sticks;
- braids and bibs of different colours (4 sets);
- 30 skipping ropes (various sizes);
- 30 hoops (60 cm and 90 cm);
- 20 plastic cones and 20 domes plus plastic flags for markers;
- nets/bins/wire baskets for holding balls, etc;
- games equipment trolley;
- trolley for hoops;
- playground chalk;
- stopwatches.

Further reading (and addresses) for games

Brown, A: *Active games for Children with Movement Problems* (Chapman, 1990)

Cooper, A: *Development of Games and Athletic Skills* (Simon & Schuster, 1992)

Severs, J: *Activities for PE* (Blackwell, 1991)

Sleap, M: *Mini-sports* (Heinemann, 1984)

Wetton, P: Bright Ideas: *Games for PE* (Scholastic Press, 1992)

Mini Hockey Rules: Hockey Association, Coaching Office, 6 St John's, Worcester WR2 5AH

Netball Rules for Young Players: All England Netball Association

Guide to Teaching Soccer in Schools: English Schools Football Association, 22 The Broadway, Darkes Lane, Potters Bar, Hertfordshire EM6 4HW

Kwik Cricket: Marylebone Cricket Club, St John's Wood, London NW8

New Image Rugby: Rugby Football Union, Twickenham TW2 1DZ

Introduction to Short Tennis for Teachers: Lawn Tennis Association, Barras Court, West Kensington, London W4 5EQ

PE Games Skills Award (available from PE Association above)

Athletics

The following is a list of suggested resources for athletics:

- A large field, or a playground area, preferably marked for games and athletic activities (see figures 35 and 36).
- Batons, plastic or wood shapes or beanbags for relays.
- Stopwatches, timers and measuring tapes.

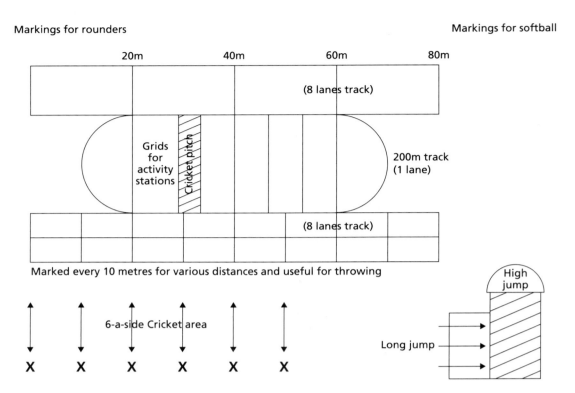

Fig 35: markings for field athletics

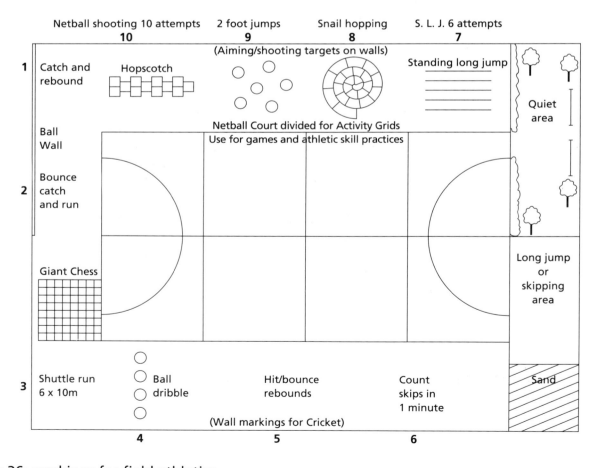

Fig 36: markings for field athletics

- Skittles and canes for jumping and hurdling (light, folding hurdles are also available).
- Jumping areas (see figures 35 and 36).
- A landing mattress (not gymnastic crash mat) for high jumping for years 5 and 6.
- Skipping ropes (various sizes).
- Cones (various sizes).
- Balls for throwing, eg large balls, tennis-sized, cricket and rounders balls.
- Foam shot, discus, javelin for juniors (see Eveque Leisure Equipment).

Useful addresses

IBM Ten Step Award Scheme: Mr L Emmence, 'Prosit', Rosedown Road, Medstead, Alton, Hampshire GU34 5LG.

English Schools Athletics Association (ESAA) Award Scheme, c/o Mr N Dickinson, 26 Coniscliffe Road, Stanley, County Durham DH9 7RF

Davies, The Sports People, c/o NES/Arnold, Ludlow Hilll Road, West Bridgford, Nottingham NC2 6HD

ASCO Education Supplies, ASCO House 19 Lockwood Way, Parkside Lane, Leeds LS11 5TH

Eveque Leisure Equipment, Dock Road, Northwich, Cheshire CW9 5HO

Resources for swimming

- Learner pool which contains shallow water and deep water.
- Buoyancy aids: a variety of plastic/rubber balls, rings and shapes, inflatable armbands and rings, sufficient floatboards for each child and extra swimming caps.

Other useful equipment for teaching swimming and diving includes diving bricks, hoops (and weighted stands), diving discs, weighted toys, and light plastic balls.

Further reading

ASA and STA Handbooks (see Resources p00), or the ASA's *Swimming Teaching and Coaching Level 1* and *Handbook for the Teacher of Swimming* (Pelham Books); *Enjoy Swimming* (Faber & Faber); *Swimming Games and Activities* (A&C Black).

Resources for outdoor and adventurous activities

Department for Education (see *Safety in Outdoor Education* (HMSO 1989)).

- Local maps, school site plans, Ordnance Survey maps of local areas to be visited.
- List of local parks, outdoor spaces, adventure playgrounds, sports clubs, etc.
- Compasses (Silva).
- Clipboards.
- Stopwatches.
- Trail markers, eg, plastic flags, cones, playground chalk, signs, etc.
- Environmental study equipment, eg, nets, pond-dippers, containers, magnifiers, etc.
- Camping equipment: small tents, basic cooking equipment and utensils.
- Sketching materials, texture rubbing materials.
- Camera, video camera.

Further reading
DES: *Learning Out of Doors* (1985, HMSO)
DES: *Safety in Outdoor Education* (1989, HMSO)
DES: *Playground Safety Guidelines* (1992, HMSO)
NCC: *Geography in the National Curriculum* (1992, Scholastic)
Bright Ideas: *The Outdoor Classroom* (1992, Scholastic)
M Cotton: *Outdoor Adventure for Handicapped People*
    (1983 Souvenir Press)

Suppliers of PE equipment
include the following:

Hestair Hope
St Phillips Drive
Royston
Oldham CL2 6AG

Evans
Mercury House
Sutherland Road
Longton ST3 1JD

NES (Davies)
17 Ludlow Hill Road
West Bridgford
Nottingham NG2 6HD

ASCO Education
ASCO House
19 Lockwood way
Parkside Lane
Leeds LD11 5TH

Sutcliffe Leisure
Sandbeds Trading Estate
Dewsbury road
Ossett
West Yorkshire WF5 9ND

Useful starter packs for all games are available from Sutcliffe Leisure.

Index